THE GLITCH

JESSICA LEWIS

authorHOUSE®

AuthorHouse™
1663 Liberty Drive
Bloomington, IN 47403
www.authorhouse.com
Phone: 1 (800) 839-8640

This book is a work of non-fiction. Unless otherwise noted, the author and the publisher
make no explicit guarantees as to the accuracy of the information contained in this book
and in some cases, names of people and places have been altered to protect their privacy.

Published by AuthorHouse   03/14/2016

ISBN: 978-1-5049-2028-5 (sc)
ISBN: 978-1-5049-2027-8 (e)

Library of Congress Control Number: 2015910436

Print information available on the last page.

Any people depicted in stock imagery provided by Thinkstock are models,
and such images are being used for illustrative purposes only.
Certain stock imagery © Thinkstock.

This book is printed on acid-free paper.

Because of the dynamic nature of the Internet, any web addresses or links contained in
this book may have changed since publication and may no longer be valid. The views
expressed in this work are solely those of the author and do not necessarily reflect the
views of the publisher, and the publisher hereby disclaims any responsibility for them.

The story you are about to read is real. All the characters and places in this book are real but all the names have been changed. This is to help protect the innocent although nobody is really innocent.

CONTENTS

CHAPTER 1

Like two friends that have not seen each other in forever just sitting around having a few drinks while we catch up. Now I know sometimes I rattle for a few minutes but I always come back to the point. So let's grab a bottle and shot glasses and get started. Forgive me if I add stuff in every now and then but as my friend you know I like to add little tid-bits of my thinking to my stories when I tell them.

Michael, my husband, is the love of my life. He is my soul mate. Michael and I have been together for 17 years and it has been a roller coaster ride of ups and downs and scary fast curves. The movie Parenthood which stars Steve Martin comes to mind. In this movie he is trying to navigate through life the best way he knows how dealing with kids, a job, in-laws and well… life. In one scene Helen Shaw who played the grandmother talked about how she loved roller coasters because she loved all the ups and downs and how it was an exciting ride. Like life, if you only ride the merry-go-round you don't get much out of it and life can be rather boring. So I think the best place to start is at the beginning so let me start with a bit of background for you so you will better understand my story.

Michael and I don't have a conventional marriage like everyone else. You can defiantly say that ours is a roller coaster full of ups and downs and fast curves. Some of the unexpected curves I could do without but because of the outcome I keep riding the ride. Or maybe it is because I am a glutton for punishment…who knows.

We have 2 beautiful daughters and an even better grandbaby. Everyone tells you that the reason grandkids are so much fun is because you can hype them all up on sugar or buy them noisy toys and send them home. I disagree with this because of something a woman at work once told me. It is the little things that as grandparents we can enjoy that we couldn't with our own kids because of the rat race of raising them. You can enjoy them acting crazy by singing and dancing with their pants on their head instead of being worried you are running late.

The day to day grind of life can become mundane and boring and sometimes that is the type of marriage Michael and I have. I have figured out through all this there are different parts to a relationship. There is the bla everyday part that deals with kids, bills, work; you know all the bullshit stuff that goes on every day. Then there is the adult time where you focus just on each other such as date night, moments stole from the day just to sit and talk to your other half or the lunch away from the kids. This is where you can have adult conversation were none of the conversation has anything to do with the bla stuff in life. Then there is the sex or romance. The intimate time between the two of you that keeps you connected on a deeper level. This isn't where you look lovingly into their eyes it is where you two are having fun. You know the likes of the other person so the sex is amazing. The connection between the two of you is something you cannot describe.

This brings me to why I'm writing this book. Several years ago I began to write my thoughts and feelings down to help me through some of our more curvy parts of the ride. Michael is my soul mate this is true. I am the female version of him and he is the male version of me. Together we are a force to be reckoned with. Michael says I am Hera to his Zeus and the rest of the worlds are mere mortals. This makes me all warm and fuzzy inside because it is so true. I even smile now thinking about when he said it to me. I told him that was one of the nicest things he ever said to me.

Even though we are close and talk about everything it can be difficult to say everything you want to say because of how it will affect the other person. You never want to speak from anger because you can't take back the things you say and for us that can be hard to do. We are both very dominant people and we both have an evil streak. The curve I am talking about can be a very dangerous curve. When you have nobody to talk to; to help you work through things ensuring you're not off your rocker or being over dramatic; it makes things hard. So I chose to write this because it helped me work through the problems or issues I am having.

To understand me better let me start by explaining a bit about my upbringing. My dad was not around much when I was growing up. He worked a lot. There are very few memories I have of my dad. I remember getting donuts once or twice as a child at a donut shop where all the police officers hung out…he taught me to ride a bike…how to fire a gun. I remember mom getting up and fixing him and his friend's breakfast before they went deer hunting. If that wasn't bad enough he would snap his fingers at my mom and she would get up and do what he asked. Every time I heard this I would cringe. He showed me that I would never take shit like that from my husband. He has sense come around. He and I don't talk that often but I know he loves me and he knows how he raised me was wrong.

Although my mom showed me how to be a very loving and caring mother who would do anything for her children she also showed me that I never wanted to be weak. She allowed my dad to get by with all the things he did to her. I always wanted my mom to step up and smack the shit out of him but she never did. After dad cheated on her and left she met a man who I saw doing the same things to her. In my opinion both were trying to control her but in different ways.

He tried stepping in and being our dad. I wanted nothing to do with that. I didn't understand why mom would put up with that from someone else like she did dad. I had no respect for him. I was sitting in the living room one day and he started to talk to me like he was my dad. I blew him off to which he said…"You don't like me…I don't like you…we just won't talk." We didn't talk for the next few years. I was fine with this because he was right I didn't like him for many reasons but the biggest one was the way I saw him treating my mom. I wanted my mom to stand up for herself. Her behavior made me mad at her. My mom is my mom and I am me…so it is what it is.

As I got older mom described me as a viper. Quiet and always watching everything while in deep thought. A beautiful snake which was nice as could be until you tried to touch it and then I would strike you dead. I saw that as being strong and standing up for myself. Making sure I stopped anyone from taking advantage of me.

I had two very strong women that played a big part in my life while I was growing up. My grandma's were rocks. They both had different ways of dealing with things but those were two women you didn't want to cross. I called one of them Grandma and the other Nanny. They both played a huge part in shaping who I am today. I spent a lot of time with them because mom didn't feel it was a good idea for me to be around my siblings. I had anger issues. I only had them at home because with my grandparents I was fine.

My Grandma showed me how to love life. She was so full of energy. Her smile and personality was contagious. Even as a small child she encouraged my creativity by listening to all my crazy stories. She would help me build forts in the living room. We would sit up late at night watching old movies and eat popcorn in the fort.

Two of my favorite memories about Grandma is how we would slide around the kitchen in our socks pretending we were ice skating and when I would help her clean. She would turn the music up so loud and we would sing and dance around while we cleaned. I still do this today...sometimes to her favorite singer...Tommy Roe.

My humor also came from her. I can explain better with a story. Grandma would let me play in the attic with her china dolls. One day we tried to pull down the attic door but it was stuck. Grandma called someone to come out and fix the door. When he arrived Grandma showed him to where the attic door was. Grandma watched from the top of the steps and I watched from the bottom. The guy set up his ladder at the edge of steps and pulled on the string but nothing happened. He pulled a bit harder and it didn't budge. He shifted on the ladder and pulled harder on the string and the string broke. This made him and the ladder topple head over heels down the stairs landing at the bottom tied in a pretzel with the ladder being part of his body. Grandma and I just about peed ourselves. I heard from upstairs through the laughter...Are you ok? She was amazing. That's why when I tricked my cousin into walking over a yellow jackets nest that I had pissed off and he was screaming and running through the yard stripping off his clothes she stood there beside me laughing. Well until she saw him swelling up and having a hard time breathing.

In the end I remember that her love for life helped her after her stroke. She went on to help others recover and get their life back after their strokes. I wanted to go and see her one time when I came home to visit but couldn't find a ride. I talked to her for hours on the phone where she told me she was going to have surgery on her kidneys to remove a stone. After I got back to where I was living I got a phone call from my mom telling me Grandma didn't make it out of surgery. I was devastated. When I walked through my front door to where I was staying the lady I was renting the room from said I had a post card from Grandma. She must have sent it the day I talked to her because she told me not to worry about the surgery and that she loved me so much. She also told me she was proud of me for living my life and following my dreams. I was around the age 18 when she died. I lost two weeks because I was devastated…my heart was broke.

Nanny was an amazing woman too. She showed me how to relax and appreciate the quiet of the world. When I was young she and Pop lived in the last house on a dirt road way out in the country. Actually if you drove another 2 minutes you would run into the River. She and I would walk the rail road tracks and flatten pennies. We would lay enough pennies on the tracks so we were sure to find a few. Sometimes we would find most of them other times we wouldn't. Over the years my collection of flattened pennies became very large.

Every year Pop would go into town and buy slag. What I liked about slag is because it had a nice mix between rocks, broken concrete and sea shells. He would use this to put down on his road and driveway so it wouldn't wash away. Nanny and I would walk down the road after he would do this and find the shells. I would tell Nanny that one day I was going to live at the beach where I could pick up sea shells anytime I wanted to. I always told her she was coming with me. We would talk about being beach bums and living in a little lean-to that we made out of palm leaves. We would fish for our dinner. I miss talking to her.

One day when I was about 8 we were canning tomatoes in the kitchen when Pop walked up to her and nibbled on her neck. She moved away from him saying not in front of and motioned to me. Pop kissed her on the check and walked out of the room. Nanny turned to me after he was gone and said…Men always want a lady in public but the bedroom is another story. Of course at the time I had no idea what that meant but trust me I do now.

She is the reason I look at marriage the way I do. You can have arguments but you work them out privately. Nobody needs to be in your marriage but the two of you. When you put each other first then you have nothing to worry about. When you include to many people in your marriage you are going to be sorry. The only people that matter are the two of you.

When I was in my 1st year of high school my mom woke me up and told me that Nanny had died in her sleep last night. The world stopped for me. The next thing I remember is standing in my bedroom window yelling at the ambulance coming up the hill to turn on their lights. Mom sent me to school that day but all I remember in my foggy state are bits and pieces of a friend of mine finding me on a bench in front of my school where he says I was just mumbling…why they didn't turn their lights on. He took me back to his house, which I don't remember. I found out later that he and his friends came to check on me throughout the day.

When my friend got home from school he took me home. I walked in the front door and right out the back and took off over the hill to Pops' house. Mom caught me at the edge of his yard and told me to stop Pop didn't need to see me like this. As soon as I walked in the house Pop said there is my girl and made Aunt Dana move. I never left his side the rest of the day.

At her funeral Pop introduced me to a gentleman saying this is my granddaughter. She is my…Babe. I just stood there. That was the only name I ever heard Pop call Nanny. I couldn't believe he called me that. He took my hand and continued to introduce me to other people. I was honored that he called me by the name he had lovingly given her but it took everything in me not to break down and cry. Pop told me I was riding in the limo with him and for me to go and tell my mom. I walked over to where my mom was standing talking to my Aunt Dana and my cousins. I told my mom that I was riding in the limo with Pop when Aunt Dana told me I had no business riding in the limo because it was for family. Hearing her say I wasn't family sent a shot through me like lightning. I wanted to rip her throat out. How dare her say I wasn't family. My cousin caught me in a midair lunging for her. I was going to kick her ass for saying I wasn't family. Still pisses me off.

At her grave site when everyone had left I walked over and put my hand on her stone. I was not a very religious person but I said a small prayer and asked God to take care of her. You all may think I am crazy but at that exact second a ray of sunshine broke through the clouds right onto her stone. A very warm feeling fell over me and I was at peace. I rubbed my hand on her stone and began to smile as a tear ran down my face. Pop asked me why I was smiling and I told him that Nanny was in heaven and she was ok. He just put his arm around me and we stood there for a very long time.

I think the biggest part of my personality came from my Pop. I remember spending a lot of time with him. Nobody liked him very much but I loved him to my very core. He had issues with my mom. In the past Pop had said he wasn't sure she was his. She was because I know my Grandma but Pop can have tunnel vision on things sometimes. He and my mom were never close. When I was born, though, he was so proud to be a Grandfather even though he technically already had two but those were Aunt Sally's kids and he always looked down on her. He and mom still were never really close but he showed me the world.

Like I said he had tunnel vision. Once he made his mind on how things were there was no changing it. He saw things his way and no other. For him to change his mind it took an act of God. I can be like that. You better have a strong opinion and a way to convince me to change my mind with proof or give it up. I trust myself and how I feel.

Come to think of it when my first daughter was born he came to see her in the hospital when he never went to the hospital to see anyone. Pop actually came to visit me in all the states I moved to. The last time he came to see me was after my second little girl was born. The doctor told him that he was not healthy enough to travel but he did what he wanted to. Pop was stubborn like that and extremely bullheaded because you didn't tell him what he could or could not do. I am so that way today. Do not tell me what I can and cannot do…you can ask me if I would like to do something but do not ever tell me.

People said my Pop was a bully and an ass but that is not how I saw him at all. He stood up for what he believed and didn't take shit from anyone and that is why I fashioned myself after him. I idolized my behaviors after him. People said Pop had an air of being better than everyone. He had a very strong sense of pride. He always told me to walk with my head up and shoulders square. He told me that when you shake someone's hand you get a firm grip and look them in the eye. This will show the world you don't take shit from anyone. He always said if you show weakness people will take advantage of you so don't give them an inch. I never did.

CHAPTER 2

My teen years are where my life fell apart. After Dad left and my moms' new boyfriend stepped in my life changed. My Grandma had moved away after her stroke to live with her sister in another state, Nanny had died, and Pop was trying his best to piece together his life. So I was on my own.

I lost interest in school. When I put forth the effort in school it came easy to me but now I didn't care. I started skipping school more than going. I began to hate the idea of anyone telling me what to do. My mom tried to reach me at one point and had my Aunt Cindy move in. She was my dads' sister but she was no help. I wasn't sure how someone who was self-centered and partied all the time was going to help but at least she was someone to talk to. She tried talking to me but all I wanted to do was leave. Listening to her stories made me want to travel and I knew where I wanted to go… the beach.

Every year dad would take us to the beach for a family reunion type vacation. The vacations set my fate though. I remember seeing the ocean for the first time. I was young but it took my breath away. I instantly felt complete…at home. From the time I woke up in the morning until they dragged me in at night I was on the beach. I loved it!! If you have never been there…go. If you have then you should understand the awe-inspiring connection you feel when you are sitting there just looking out over the water.

Anyway so I started spending time in my dads' parents' house. To let you know what they were like is easy my Mamaw was in the Who's Who of American Business Women. She was more into her career and what she had than anything else. Papaw was more down to earth. I got along better with him then I did her.

She wanted me to become a lawyer because she said I could argue with anyone. I was good at it. I could manipulate people into a corner so they really did not have an out. My point of view was the only one that mattered. This would make her so mad because she would finally just move on and stop talking to me. I wanted to be a journalist that traveled the world. I wanted to be the one who exposes all the bad in the world.

I started spending more time at their house because, at the time, my favorite Aunt Monica had moved in after her husband died in a fire. I had spent a week with her after one of our family reunions when I was younger. She took me out to a pizza place and let me drink beer. I found that exciting even though I didn't really like the taste of beer. She never treated me like a kid and I liked that. She never told me what to do. She was only about 10 years older than me so I looked up to her.

One afternoon I was at my dad's parents' house downstairs when my aunts came in and locked the door. They pulled out the hide away bed and began to pull some green stuff out of a baggy. Aunt Monica turned to me and asked if I wanted to join them. I got up and walked over and sat on the bed with them. The first joint we smoked did nothing to me but the second sure did. The three of us sat there and laughed. They began telling me stories which made me feel included. This was a feeling I had not felt in a long time. This was my first experience in the drug scene. I was 14. They introduced me to a lot of drugs that summer.

One night at my moms' house I called a guy who I knew had some pot and asked him to come over. My mom was out with her boyfriend and my sister and brother were asleep so we went upstairs to my room to get high. We sat around talking and listening to music. When I realized it was 1am I knew my mom would be home soon. We started heading downstairs when I heard her pull into the driveway so we ran back upstairs. I told him I was going to lay down because she would come up and check on us. I told him when she went to bed I would sneak him out of the house.

The night turned ugly fast. I woke up to a knife to my throat and him sliding in. Until this event I was a virgin but he forcibly took that part of me. I still have the scar under my chin to prove it. I had lost everything in my life that was important to me and now this. I am not sure how to explain what this did to me. You feel dirty and ashamed. You know in your head that everyone is looking at you now because they know. Your body feels different in the way you walk. You want to die. You feel so many emotions. The black hole that you fall in warps your thinking.

I had told my best friend and she told me that I needed to get checked. I didn't even know what that meant. She told me to call my aunt and tell her that I needed to get the pill because of cramps. I called my Aunt Monica and she had no problem taking me. I told her what my best friend told me to tell her because now there was more on my mind than just being pregnant. After talking to my best friend I wanted to make sure he didn't give me a STD or make me pregnant. I was scared. I never told her the real reason because I was ashamed.

My mom never knew what happened to me. Maybe if I had told her things would have been different but because of the way I was and because I had invited him I figured that she would not have believed me. I became very private after this. Drugs became a very big part of my life. I would hide my stash in the album covers on my wall and in a bag tucked away in my closet. I came home one day from school and my moms' boyfriend was sitting on the couch. All he said to me when I walked in the room was, "We told you to clean your room." I went upstairs to find that my mom had cleaned my room. I was pissed. I don't remember what happened next but she told me I backed her up against the wall by her throat and when she told me I would go to jail if I hurt her I guess I told her that was fine I would get out when I was 18.

She called my dad the same day and he moved me into his house the next day. She didn't know what else she could do and she figured he could help me...she was wrong. Dad, I guess tried but I was to far gone by now. I had lost everyone that was important to me including me. I remember one time shortly after I moved in with my dad he found pot and birth control pills in my purse. I lied and told him I was holding the pot for someone else but the pills had my name on them. He took away my birth control and gave me back the pot. I laughed to myself; I guess my dad wants a pregnant high daughter. He left for work and I called my aunt and told her I needed to go back to the clinic to get more pills while I smoked a joint on the back porch. His behavior that day stunned me.

I really began to get into drugs and drinking. I was always high, drunk or on something....sometimes all at the same time. Amphetamines were my pill of choice because I needed something to help me stay awake. I began to party hard that year.

That summer my aunts threw some great parties which I was invited to come to after I had put her kids to sleep. All these parties happened when Mamaw would go out of town. She traveled a lot with her job and would be gone for sometimes a week at a time. During this time Papaw would drink and I mean drink. He always forgot to pick her up at the airport. When she would get home we would play a game of what I liked to call Find Papaw. See Papaw would tell me where he was going and when she would come looking for him I was to call the bar so he could leave. He would come back to the house and tell me where he was going next. She always came back home to see if he was there. Like clockwork this is what would happen and every time she would come home I would just say, "No I haven't seen him", and off she would go again.

The next day though when she was at work he would do something so over the top it was obvious what he was doing. One time he built a shed in the back yard. I have never seen a man clean an entire house so thoroughly before in my life. Dinner let me tell you about the dinners he would have ready when she got home...WOW. She would forgive him every time. It didn't make sense to me then but now I understand. She allowed him to break away while she was gone so that they could be closer when she was home. Funny, how in retrospect, I was watching me in the future. Not exactly but in a way it was.

It had been about a year now from the time I was rapped when I met the next man who would seal my ideas on sex. He was about 7 or 8 years older than me; I was about to turn 16 at the end of the summer. He was tall, well-built, blonde hair, blue eyes, tanned and he was the best looking guy I had ever met. Looking back now I know that he was a snake in the grass. Men like him are the kind of men I warn my daughters about.

I never had anyone to warn me about men like him so I bought all his bullshit, hook line and sinker. He listened to me and took an interest in what I had to say. The way he explained about keeping our dating a secret because of his age and people wouldn't understand made sense to me so I kept it a secret. I began to share my rape story with him and he acted like it killed him that someone would do that to me, when he told me he loved me...I bought it all. He made all my walls drop because he knew just what

11

to say and how to say it. After a bit he began to subtly hint about sex and how I should know what it was like to be with someone who loved me to erase all those bad memories. I finally gave in and he walked away. I was devastated and in my opinion I was raped all over again.

Trust me when I say this cut me to my core and caused me to turn into a real viper. My first time I was rapped and the second time I bought into all the lies and gave in. This would never happen again. I threw up all my walls and created a safe place for myself by taking on the philosophy that… if this is what men truly want and can do and say anything to get their way then I could do the same. No lies…no BS if you were good enough to get in my pants count yourself lucky but don't ever think you're the only one and don't think you will get away without scars. I was going to get what I wanted and I didn't care who I hurt in the process. They didn't.

My dad handed me over to my aunt which was what I wanted because she let me do anything I wanted to do. She would pay me in pot to babysit her kids. I skipped school anytime I wanted to. My aunt got a wild hair up her butt and would take off drinking for a few days; one time she took off to the beach and left me with her kids for a week. I was cool with that because when she got back we talked my dad into letting me move to the beach with her.

I was ready to go. I couldn't wait to see the ocean, feel the sand on my feet, the salty wind air in my face. I wanted to go and sit on the beach and find myself again. Sadly though, she didn't move anywhere I could see the beach. It was ok at least I knew it was just 15 minutes away. When I saw the ocean again I got tears in my eyes. I felt a calming peaceful feeling swept over me and while everyone else played on the beach I just sat there all day watching the ocean.

Within my first month I saw an alligator eat the neighbor's dog. I was laying out getting sun when our neighbors' dog started going nuts. I looked up to see the alligator heading right for the dog. I stared in disbelief for a moment before I jumped up and called the police but by the time they arrived the dog was dead and the alligator was sunning itself on the neighbors' porch.

I was in my last year of high school. One day sitting in class I heard some of the people in class talking about a concert going on at the beach at the band shelter. They said Joan Jet was going to be there and I loved her music. I looked out the window and felt as though I was suffocating. I was not living life the way I wanted to. Here I was sitting in class wasting away when there was so much life going on just on the other side of the window. I stood up and started to walk out when the teacher asked where I was going. I handed her my books and said to the beach to see Joan Jett and I walked out the door never to return. On a side note I went and got my GED less than a year later and scored very high.

The concert was awesome. I had a blast. I got high all day listening to great music. I danced on the beach and singing all the songs with the crowd. All the loneliness drifted away. I was in a world of my own. I love music and today I was on the beach with the wind in my hair listening to one of my favorite singer. You cannot imagine the freedom I felt that day. It was one of the best days I had experienced in a long time. It was amazing to see her. This was my first concert and I couldn't ask for more. I couldn't wait to get back to my aunts' house to tell her.

The bullshit I walked into when I got back to my aunts' dumbfounded me. I walked in the door all prepared to tell my aunt about my kick ass day on the beach when she started in on me. My school had called and told her what I had done. She began to yell and scream at me telling me that I had no right ditching school and going to the beach. She went on to say all these 'what if' scenarios that didn't seem to bother her when she was the one out running around doing what she wanted to do. I saw her as a hypocrite and a controlling bitch. She wanted me to be her baby sitter so she could come and go as she pleased and didn't want me to live my life. How was she going to try and parent me now after all I had been allowed to do? So I cut her off mid yell and told her that she wasn't my mom and how dare she take this tone when she had let me skip school anytime I wanted and paid me in pot to baby sit her kids for years. I walked into my room packed my backpack with what was most important to me and walked out the door.

This really ended our relationship. I spent some time with her a bit later but things were never the same. I looked at her differently. To me she was my best friend and she turned into an adult like everyone else. To me with all she had done she didn't have a leg to stand on to judge my behavior or the things I wanted to do. I wish things would have gone differently but they didn't so there is no use crying over spilt milk.

CHAPTER 3

The next 8 years was a mix between business, pleasure and lost time. I had many jobs over the 8 years but I was on my own. Each one of them had unique advantages to them. All of them were fun even if they were not fun jobs. I met a lot of people while I was working. I have many good memories of things I did during that time.

One of the jobs I had during this time was selling sun tan lotion for a company. The advantage of this job was that I got to walk up and down the beach in my bikini and work on my tan while I made money. The man that hired me ran a little shop on the beach. I was walking on the beach one day when he yelled at me and said he wanted to talk to me. When I walked over he began to explain that I was exactly what they were looking for. He thought I would make a lot of money selling sun tan lotion to tourist.

Now I'm thinking … walk up and down the beach in my bikini and flirt … oh yea I can do that. This was the best job I ever had. I personally used the products so they could see how well it worked. One of the biggest pick-up lines men used was about my tan telling me that they would like to lick my tan skin to find the creamy center. They compared me to a milky piece of chocolate. Yes this job was fun and I got all my stuff for free so I took the job.

I did very well because what man can turn down someone who is tall, well-built, long blonde hair that just touch the top of my butt, and a deep golden brown tan. I didn't find any. Now the woman with them got a bit bent by me but they were easy enough to maneuver around. I mainly went after the group of guys that most women wouldn't give the time of day because I knew I could sell to them. A bit of flirting and they were hooked.

I remember walking around one day when I saw a group of guys standing around trying to pick up girls. They were not what I really noticed though. I noticed the scrawny, unkempt haired and not very attractive boy in the back wiping off the car the other guys were sitting on. I watched for a minute and saw that he was the money behind the spring trip vacation and that was all he was to these guys a means to an end. That did not sit well with me because I cannot stand bullies. I watched how they yelled and said get me a beer and he would do it. I knew what I was going to do. It was towards the end of the day and I was ready for the night to begin.

I walked up to the group and walked right past the ones in front to the guy in the back. I began to talk to him about buying sun tan lotion. I knew as soon as I started his friends would jump in and they did. I made them spend their money which I found enjoyable. When I had gotten all the guys to buy something I asked the unattractive one if he would like to party with me and my friends that night. His friends all said yes but were dumbfounded when I curled my nose at them and said that I wasn't talking to them I was talking to the attractive guy in the group. The guy I was talking to acted like I was speaking a foreign language and kept trying to redirect me to his friends. I told him no he was the one I wanted and that I would pick him up at 9.

I left and told 4 of my girlfriends what we were going to do that night and why. I explained the situation and told them my plan. They were more than happy to help. We put on our best going out clothes...which wasn't much at all and headed out. His friend answered the door and once again tried to hit on us. I do not remember the lame comments but trust me I have heard better pick-up lines from a monkey. His friends figured we would never show. One of the guys said I guess I owe you $50 and one of my friends walked over to him took the $50 and said, "First round of drinks is on this looser".

We had a good time. All the drinks were for free and we each took turns dancing with him. I watched him throughout the night and could see that he was enjoying himself. We went to an after-hours party when the bar closed and I introduced him to everyone as my cousin and he was treated with respect. Something I could see that did not happen very often. We all danced with him and drank till dawn. Sitting on the beach we watched the sun rise when he turned to me and said thank you for everything. I told him he was a nice guy and that he needed to stand up to his so called friends. I further said if he didn't stand up for himself then nobody would. I took him back to the hotel and handed him the underwear I had collected from the girls and told him to make the story good. He just smiled and said that this was the best night of his life and thank you. I still smile when I think of that night and wonder what he is doing now.

I often wonder where some of the people are that I have known in my past. One person I wonder about is Tommy. I met him when I worked at a beach burger place. It sat right off the beach. I know that I didn't spend a lot of time with him but the time that I did was great. Tommy was the first gay guy I had ever met. He was short, kind of heavy with blondish red hair, and so overtly gay acting. You know like most characters you see on TV that was him. He had a heart of gold though and a smile that would not stop.

I remember coming to work one day tripping on acid. Tommy said hello to me but in my altered state I thought it was a parrot. To his amusement I began looking for a bird. When I wasn't looking he would say it again which made me look even harder. After about 15 min he busted out laughing and said it again so I could see him. He and I just laughed about that for the rest of the day. We would stand behind the counter and talk about people walking by. I actually met my ex-husband through Tommy but I will mention my x later. Sometimes we would play a game when we were bored at work called "I could get him" this is where we would bet on who would be able to sleep with the guy we saw walking down the boardwalk…believe it or not he was right sometimes which shocked the shit out of me. He would turn up with one of the guys we saw walking by that day with a big smile on his face and all I could do is shake my head. Tommy was a good friend of mine and I really miss him.

I knew lots of people but did not have many friends. When you live the life I did you learn trust is a luxury that I couldn't afford. Sadly, this meant I didn't trust anyone. You couldn't trust people just to be your friends without wanting something from you. Everyone I knew had a story to tell. Some of those stories were really sad and others well … their choices brought on their life situations. I don't have sympathy for people like that especially when all they do is bitch and do not try and fix anything for the better.

Not trusting people made it very hard to get close to anyone. I found that when you let people in it is easier for them to hurt you. This is why I spent a lot of time alone. I found it easier to rely on myself then to count on anyone else. To many people in your business means your business is open for discussion and some of my business was just that ... MY BUISNESS.

My business was not always legal. I never did anything I thought was immoral, you know like prostitution, but everything else was fair game. I know there is or was a government file on me and that I was watched during a portion of my wild days and even after I settled down for a bit. It wouldn't have mattered if I did get questioned by the authorities because I was smart enough to not ask questions and I kept my head down so that I couldn't have described anyone anyway. Well, I could have told them they wore nice shoes and they were black but that was it. I never told anyone about the things I did. I felt the more people that knew my business the more likely I was to get caught. There were only 2 people in my inner circle and that was only because I needed them. That is all I feel I can say about these things since I'm not entirely sure that the statute of limitations has run out on me. So until then...if you can imagine it I probably did it...at least in one form or another.

There are times I often wondered what happened to the people I met when I lived on the beach. Many years later after that life I had a gentlemen walk into the convenient store I was running who told me he remembered me. We talked about a few of the people I had known and he told me that some were no longer with us. That saddens me... we were not all that close but it is sad I got out and they didn't. I remember many nights sitting around drinking with them. For 8 years of my life they were, for lack of a better term, my family. So for the ones I do not know about I will continue to believe they are somewhere nice and have a good life.

Sex was a big part of my party time. Now remember what I thought about sex. I didn't even need to know their names if I wanted them that was all that mattered. If they acted like they were getting attached I moved on. I remember one spring break I was working at a fish restaurant when I heard and saw this nice bike pull up. A well-built man got off of the bike. I turned to the guy I was working with and told him if the face matches the body I was out of here. Needless to say it did and I picked him up. He gave me a ride home and we spent the week together. I really enjoyed that week.

I received a letter from him which said in short if the girls were like me back where I came from the boys were very happy.

Now my off times were great. After I moved out of my aunts' house Pop came down to surprise me. I got a call at work from my mom asking me when I got off work that day. I asked her why and she said I had a surprise coming. Just then Pop walked through the door with my sister and cousin. I was so happy to see him. I took them back to my one bedroom apartment. I had forgotten that my Aunt, who I was talking to again, had come over and left some pot on my kitchen counter. I am glad my sister was watching out for me and put all my pot in one of my kitchen drawers so Pop wouldn't see.

I had forgotten that there was a party at my house that night. Pop had a good time drinking with the people that came. The next day when we woke up we all went to the beach. It was funny listening to Pop talk about all the girls in their suits or lack thereof. That night I told my sister I would take her out to the party I was invited to. Pop told me not to get her drunk and let her go swimming. I agreed and headed out for the night to get my sister drunk and have a good time. I was forced to take my cousin. This turned out as a really bad idea since she threw up on my friends white carpet because she couldn't hold her alcohol like she said she could. As we all got back to my apartment my sister wanted to go swimming probably because she liked one of the guys that came with us. My cousin just passed out on the beach chair and I ended up having sex in the hot tub with the other guy.

The next morning when we woke up I noticed Pop was skinned all the way up his arm. When I asked him about it this is what he told me. He explained that he was outside minding his own business drinking his second drink of the night when all of a sudden he heard a noise and the next thing that happened was the bushes jumped out and attacked him. He actually said all of that with a straight face. I asked him where the bottle of Rum was and he said he must have lost it.

The type of party I was accustom to were wild. I toned the one down that Pop was at but all the other ones were very memorable…even though I don't remember much. You know the parties you see on the movies those were mild compared to the parties I went to. If you are not a partier watch the movie Point Break that is how the parties started. I cannot tell you how they ended since I don't remember most of them. All I know there was music, a lot of drinking, drugs and a lot of sex. There were a few parties

I woke up the next morning where I had started the night at. The house would be wall to wall empty beer bottles, glasses, plastic baggies, bongs, pipes, mirrors on the table and half naked and naked people sleeping all over the place including the bathtub. One time I saw some pictures that were taken that night…thank goodness I was not in any of those pictures. It is safe to say anyone in those pictures cannot run for political office.

My favorite place to be was a little hole in the wall bar. It was quiet and relaxing. They had live bands that played Reggae music, so fitting the atmosphere of the bar. This is where I would go to have a good time. The bar opens up right on the beach. There were many mornings I remember waking up just outside the bar because I had passed out on the beach. The people were wonderful and their specialty drink was out of this world. Actually my favorite bar now, along with my friend and favorite bartender makes me this drink today. My old bar has since moved up in the world. So the next time you go to your favorite bar pour out a little in memory of all those who have come before you.

My life was not all fun and games. I know that I worried my family. It is nice to know they never gave up hope that I would make it out of there safe, especially my mom. In the back of my head I always knew that. I have a lot of respect for my mom because she never gave up hope. Not all the people I knew had family who believed in them. That is why they ended up forgotten and on the streets. Never lose faith in those you love because things may work out better than you know. My mom didn't she always told me I could come home but there would be rules that I would have to follow. I was just not ready for rules at that point in my life.

I was my own boss and did as I wanted to do. Yes I had bad times where I had to sleep in abandoned hotels, on the beach, even on the concrete slab under the very top of an overpass, but my life was mine and I answered to no one. Scary sometimes … yes … but they were my choices and mine alone. Nobody was responsible for me but me. Not all of those 8 years were street based but when you don't keep a permanent address for longer than a few months you might as well say streets.

The end of my wild days came the day I met my ex-husband. I told you that I would mention him and this is all I have to say about him. He gave me a beautiful little girl who became my world. We talked about having kids and I figured that it was about time. I never thought I would want kids because I saw them as a way to tie me down. Seeing her little face and tiny hands and feet I was hooked. In that split second I knew that I would move heaven and earth to protect her. On the day she was born and I saw her for the first time the world disappeared completely and all I was aware of was her. I don't understand people who give up their kids. I would go without and do anything to keep my kids safe and with me. That is why I raised her on my own until I met Michael.

After I settled down I made amends with my estranged family for all the worry and stress I caused. I felt bad for all the worries I caused my mom. I remember a Mother's Day calling her from a truck stop, I don't remember where I was, but I called to wish her a happy mommy day. When she found out I was hitchhiking she asked me to call her when I got back to my home. All in all my life is my life and it made me who I am today so I would not trade any of it.

CHAPTER 4

Michael is the man that finally caught me and melted my cold heart. He grew up half way across the country. Actually he was in a state that I never had much interest in visiting let alone moving to. When I moved out there it was only to help my sister. So this move was just a pit stop for me. She was having major marital problems and needed me to help her with the kids. So I moved away from the beach to help her.

He lived a very boring life. We came from two different worlds. You could almost say we were as different as night and day but in the end both day and night complement each other and without one you cannot have the other. His mom is nothing like my mom. His mom is very controlling on some things but not on other. She would treat any girl that came around like they were a piece of trash, a slut. Even when they were just friends or a boss that had stopped over she would have a fit and throw them out. His sister, though, could have boys in her room with the door closed. In my opinion she is a bit crazy with the way she looks at things especially the more I got to know her but more about her later and we will see if you agree.

Michael was a city boy and still is. He was an only child, his mom adopted his sister but he was already an adult by this time. Michael came from an upper middle class family where he had everything he wanted. Actually he had his bedroom and then he had another bedroom for all of his stuff. His part of the house was the entire top floor. His dad worked for a major corporation and the Air Force.

I met Michael while I worked at a major retail all in one store. He was my boss. Now I am his. Funny how that all worked out isn't it. At first I

21

didn't like him because I thought he was an ass. One day I over heard him say to a co-worker that she should sue the city and when she asked why he said for placing the sidewalk to close to her ass. I soon realized he wasn't being mean he was being rudely sarcastic, which, oddly enough, is a very attractive quality that I liked.

I met a girl there and she and I began to talk. We hit it off right from the start. She had a good personality and I didn't have any friends and she was becoming one. One day she invited me to come down to her house. When I got there I found out Michael was her roommate. Since we all worked the same schedule we all had the same days off together. At first it was her and I spending our days off together, then it became all three of us and then it was just Michael and I. This happened because she would go to bed and leave him there with me till the wee hours of the night/morning however you want to look at it.

It didn't take long for me to see that he was the one for me. I liked his humor, attitude, the way he looked at things, the way he treated me and his honesty. He and I would sit up talking and playing games. Nightmare Creatures was the first video game I ever played. I never had much use for video games. I always thought they were pointless and a colossal waste of time. It turns out I love video games. On a side note…men you want to be able to play your games in peace get your other half involved…find a game they will like…trust me once they like to play all you will have to worry about is who gets the gaming station. I had a blast. Hacking creatures into tiny pieces appealed to some twisted part of me I guess. I actually love to sit and watch the story plot in all the games Michael plays.

My little girl and I liked spending time with him. He took us to the park. One of the things they loved to do to me when we went to the park was fight. He would put her on his back and swing her around while they both pretended to fight me. We really liked the Matrix movie. Not to mention she began taking Martial Art with him. We would push her on the swings and listen to music while we threw rocks in to the water.

We spent a lot of time together. We talked about everything. We both had been married before and knew what we would and would not put up with. At first we didn't care what the other thought about what we had to say. I wasn't going to compromise and settle for less and neither was he. If I didn't like what I found out I would just leave. It was no big deal.

The more I got to know him the more I realized he was perfect for me. We agreed on everything. We wanted the same things out of life. I found myself falling in love for the first time in my life. Here was a man who made me smile even though he wasn't there. I found myself wanting to be with him. This was an odd feeling for me because I never let anyone in. The way he began to look at me made me feel the love I had wanted all my life.

He loves my independence, quick sarcastic wit, how passionate I was about my ideals and beliefs, what a good mother I was to my daughter. He knew if I treated mine that way then I would treat ours just the same. This is something he always looked for. He wanted someone to share his life with that completed him as a person and someone who he knew would be a good mother. He had wanted this since he was young. He wanted a family and I loved that about him. He even loves my; don't take crap attitude. His first wife was a needy insecure person and he hated that.

It would be late when we would decide to go to bed. I usually slept on the couch or in his recliner. That got old so I told him I thought he should let me sleep with him. He didn't care and we were not thinking about sex… well I was since it had been 5 years since I had last had sex with anyone. One night I was woke up to Michael humping my leg. I found it cute he found it slightly embarrassing and awkward when I told him the next day.

Like I told you earlier my little girl took martial arts with him. The three of us went to their promotion. I was very proud of both of them. The more time we spent together the closer the three of us became. There were some problems with our daughter not wanting to give up her mom but in the end they are as thick as thieves.

My little girl and I had just spent another wonderful weekend with Michael. We were getting ready to leave when she ran upstairs to say bye to Michael. When she came back downstairs she had a very odd look on her face. I asked her what was wrong and she looked at me with tears in her eyes and said I accidently called him daddy. Shocked, I gave her a hug and asked if she was ok. She told me yes and just stood there with a smile on her face. She told me that she wished he was her dad. I gave her another kiss and a hug and told her I was going to say good-bye and we could talk about it in the car. I was actually going upstairs to check on Michael. He was just as shocked and happy as she was. That began our life together.

We had been secretly dating for about 4 months before we told anyone. That included my daughter. She was the first one we told after that because we knew she was happy and wanted to be a family. His friends on the other hand would be different. He had a friend that was a controlling witch and had caused problems for him and his first wife. So once again she tried the same crap with me as she tried with his ex. She even went as far as to tell me something she thought was a bad thing about him. I'm sure this was to make me not want to be with him. Little did she know that I found her stories made him, well, hot. Her, on the other hand, it made her look pathetic. Michael came across like a good boy but this let me see that maybe he might have a bit of a dark side. Michael was ready this time for her and all her crap. I'm not going into this long sorted history with them because it has no bearing on anything else. Just like a bug on the window you just wipe away.

The three of us were growing closer together and it was a perfect fit. I saw the way he looked at my little girl with all the love in the world and my little girl looked at him the same. He was the first man she had ever seen me with. I don't believe that kids should watch you try people on. I feel you should keep your private life private. Until you feel that the relationship will go to the next level you should keep your kids out of it.

You know from the start the world seemed to be against us. We lost our jobs where we met. We lost all our friends. On top of that I had a doctor call me at work on my birthday to tell me I had cervical cancer. I went home and told Michael about the phone call. We talked about what we were going to do next. That night I woke up to see him sitting on the bed quietly crying because he was afraid he was going to lose me. I didn't realize how much he cared already but when I saw him crying it broke my heart and all I wanted to do is hold him. I gave him his moment alone though.

We found a specialist and took him all my paperwork. We were both very nervous we did not know what to expect. I had one beautiful daughter but we wanted one from the both of us. I knew he would love my daughter as his own and he had shown me that already but we really wanted another one.

Our prayers were answered with this doctor. I loved my doctor he was great. A perfect fit for me. He had hair like Gene Wilder in Frankenstein all crazy. He called us back into his office and explained the test results all looked normal. He was not sure why they would tell me that I had cervical cancer all women have abnormal cells in their pap test especially after they have had a period. You know how people have to study for years to be a doctor well just because they graduated does not mean they graduated at the top of the class. I guess the doctor from the clinic cheated all the way through school. Michael and I were relieved. After a long talk we decided to leave it in God's hands and if I got pregnant then I did.

We really knew from the beginning we would be together forever. Two years into our relationship Michael figured that after all this time if I hadn't changed "shown my true colors" then it was time to take the next step. He began his search for the perfect ring. He knew I didn't like diamonds and I was unique so he had to find the right one. He finally found the perfect setting and asked them to put an opal in the setting which is my favorite stone.

His next sneaky thing was to plan when and where to ask me. That Christmas he bought me an Eriquies Ingiales cd titled Escape. The song Hero is our song. He would and still does sing to me. I lie in the nook of his neck and feel the vibration on my head and listen to the sound of his voice and I love it. It makes me cry every time. Over the years he has chosen many songs for us as a couple. Lucky by Jason Mraz is the perfect song for us because over the years we have stayed each other's best friends. Another Jason Mraz song is I Won't Give Up On Us…that man sure has a way with words. He can reach right into you and pull out how you really feel. There are more but those are for other reasons.

That Christmas he took me to a cliff out in the woods overlooking the lake and proposed. I was the happiest I have ever been. I would see people get engaged on T.V. and how they all acted so sappy and I thought it was stupid but here I was in a state of uncontrollable giddiness. I really loved him. So happy in fact that when he asked I almost shoved him off a cliff, well, I was so excited that I practically jumped into his arms and he slipped and if he had slipped back any further he would have went off the cliff. The ring was perfect. I have never seen anything so beautiful. That was one of the best Christmas's of my life.

I had told him that if I wasn't pregnant by this Christmas then I didn't want to have any more kids. We had been trying but with no luck. I figured that because of my age it was just to hard. I didn't want to be in a walker when my baby graduates. I wanted to be able to enjoy them. After he purposed the thought of a baby was not a thought in my head. I was just looking forward to beginning our family, my life with the man that I was madly in love with.

The next month we found out we were pregnant. I guess when you stop trying to have a baby you get pregnant. On a funny note all my children were born in September... can you guess what I like to do when it's cold. Anyway, in August he woke me up and asked me if I wanted to get married, laughing I said sure. He told me to get up and get in the shower. When I walked downstairs there sat our friend who just happened to be a minister and we got married at the house. I cried. It was an emotional moment. Our little girl cried too. She was so happy because she finally had a dad.

This was going to be Michael's first baby and pregnancy. He always knew me to be a very dominate strong willed girl who takes no crap from anyone and now I cry. I could feel the mood hit me and there was no stopping it. I never really had morning sickness with any of my kids. The crying fits got on my nerves and Michaels' too. I remember sitting outside of a convenient store when one hit me. I looked at Michael and told him here it comes. He looked up and saw a bunch of men standing around and then he looked at me and said not here baby. The tears started and I couldn't stop them. He just took the dirty looks from people with grace and walked into the store. He just held me when I broke down at Wal-Mart. The men walking by understood though they had looks of understanding on their faces.

Our second daughter was born and from day one I knew something was wrong. My husband had to come up to the hospital just so I could get some sleep. At about a month old she was admitted into the hospital and was diagnosed with sever acid reflux. That took its toll on us because I never got any sleep. One day about a month after she was released I went to take a nap. It was not time for her medicine so I didn't give it to her. Michael thought that I did. It wasn't till later that day that we figured out that neither one of us had given it to her. She just sort of grew out of it. Thank goodness but my prayers go out to all the moms with children who have acid reflux. I found though that a small piece of peppermint before bed helped her sleep through the night.

Michael is a wonderful father even though his 1st experience with a baby was a hard one because of her issues. Her fear of water he got her over by having her help him water the plants outside until one day he had her in a little tub of water playing. He did make a huge mistake that we still talk about today though. He had her outside and put her down so he could look at his plants. He had taken his eyes off of her for a minute but when he turned around she was chewing on something. It was a slug. I know right that is so gross. She is still an odd one. She likes shrimp and chocolate ice-cream together.

One of the things I love about him is the way he loves his family. The devotion he shows in everything he does for us is a beautiful thing. I pity the person who ever comes against his family on any level. God Himself will be their only saving grace. I feel the same way about my family and because of the way we feel neither one of us worry about the world.

In my opinion, it is best to have both parents a male and a female because of the life experiences they provide. I am not saying that a gay couple cannot raise wonderful children all I am saying is that each one of the sexes brings different outlooks and advantages to the table when we talk about raising kids. Michael will let the girls grow in a way I never could. He allows them to do the daring, carefree stuff that as a mom I think is to dangerous. There are good examples of this like when Michael let our oldest jump off a bridge into a creek or how Michael thought it was no big deal when our youngest chewed on a slug. As a mom we think of...well all the scary what if situations that can harm our kids. This is all so our children stay protected. As a mom we know there are a lot of scary things in the world and we want to keep them safe as long as we can. Women are more compassionate then men so we show them how to be loving adults. I raise my girls to the best of my ability trying to instill the values that were instilled in me. To be self-reliant, strong, smart, quick thinking...all the things they need to face the big bad world while teaching them to be loving, nurturing, caring mothers someday. All moms show their daughters how to be moms or what kind of woman their little boys want to marry to make sure their kids are well taken care of.

Men are dare devils. They are more adventurous and they instill that in children too. They also teach little boys how they should treat their wives and what little girls should expect from their future husbands. Men are important parts of their daughter's lives by giving them a tree to lean on. It really does take a village to raise children and I'm sorry but I know that same sex parents can be good parents but those kids miss out on having both influences in their lives. That is my opinion though and only my opinion.

Ok sorry about the side track so I will get back with the story. So I noticed I was starting to lose my hair and I couldn't lose any weight I had gained with our youngest. Michael suggested going to see the doctor about it. The doctor decided it was best to do an ultra sound to see if maybe he could see something. The second she put that device on my stomach and we saw 2 little pockets we both had tears in our eyes. That was a shock for both of us. Michael had always felt he was supposed to have twins and now he was having them. It was a wonderful and scary day for both of us. For the next few months he and I were on cloud 9.

Unfortunately the troubles started with a pain in my side that was so bad I couldn't move or breathe. We had gone to get something to eat and I began to have a sharp pain in my side that felt like someone was sticking a knife in my side that doubled me over. Every time I tried to take a breath I couldn't. This started our journey over the next several months were I was in the hospital more than out. Our first trip to the hospital was very emotional.

Not knowing what was going on Michael and I drove to the hospital. When we got there they took me back very quickly and a female doctor came in. She did an exam which it felt like she just shoved her hand up there with no care in the world and it hurt like hell. When she was done she looked at us and said she had no idea what was going on because everything felt fine. I explained that the pain was more on my side and I couldn't breathe. All I knew was that I was in pain and the Doctor had no idea what was wrong which made me very worried. Everything was chaotic with people all talking about what was going on but nobody was talking to us but it gave me a feeling that something was really wrong. Not to mention the priest that had called Michael out of the room to discuss God with him and to seek his guidance in this tuff time which just pissed him off. I looked at Michael and started to say take care of the girls but he stopped me and told me I would be fine and he didn't want to hear any different. The look on his face said it all for me. I knew he loved me but in that split second I knew beyond a shadow of a doubt that I was his world...just like he was mine. I was admitted to the hospital for more tests. When my Doctor came in he put our minds at ease and told us that I had pneumonia and that they were going to keep me for a few days to help get me back on track.

I wish this would have been the worse things we had to go through because the next several months were hell. I would stand up and just start gushing blood where it would cover me and the floor around me up to a foot around. Each time I was taken to the hospital I was admitted for 3 or 4 days at a time. Each time they would give me an ultra-sound to check the babies. I would watch them play like they were not bothered by anything. There was one ultra-sound where I watched one of them bump into the other to which the other one bumped back and that started a bumping war inside my stomach. They were amazing to watch. The only thing I regret is that Michael could not see them. Actually Michael never got to see them like that because he was always in the room with our baby. I would tell him all about it but I knew he would have rather seen it for himself. Each time I was in the hospital he was at home with our two daughters holding down the house and trying to work. We had no help with the baby so it was all on Michaels shoulders. I was in the hospital so much that when I came home the baby would want Michael more than me.

One of our trips to the hospital was especially hard on Michael. I stood up and the blood covered me and the floor. I went to the bathroom because I was feeling cramps. When I stood up I yelled for Michael because I was afraid I had just lost one of the babies. Michael looked in the toilet and noticed a big mass covered in blood and told me to go into the living room He reached into the toilet and placed what we thought was a little sack into a baggy and helped me to the car. He was always very reassuring in everything he said to me. I could see the sadness all over his face but because he is my hero he never let me see him worry or him scared. Turns out it was just a clot but the entire ride to the hospital and until the Doctor told us what it was we just sat together quietly with him holding our baby girl who was still a handful because of her acid reflux.

The day before I lost them we were in the living room talking about how our life was going to change once they were here. He started to talk about how scared he was with all my bleeding problems so I walked over to him and he put his head on my belly. The second the boys heard his voice they rolled towards him. They almost made me lose my balance the movement was so fast. Michael felt them move for the first time. It was a very special moment. One neither of us will ever forget. As long as he talked they stayed close to him. Little did we know I would lose them the next day and that would be the first and last time Michael would feel his boys...alive. I am glad he has that moment.

April 5 became one of the worse days we have ever experienced. We had made plans to go to the Indian Fair after he got off work but instead I had to call him and let him know that I thought something was really wrong. He rushed home and put me and the baby in the car. My Doctor had left that day on vacation so I was stuck with the piece of shit doctor that was on call. They took me back and the Doctor explained to us that one of my bags had a hole in it and I was feeling contractions and that there was nothing he could do. The coldness and bland way in which he told us just pissed me off. I looked at him and asked if there was anything like give them shots of steroids so that could speed their lungs up. He just said no. I asked him if there was anything he could give me to stop the contractions. He said no and walked away. Then another priest walked in and said she wanted to talk and all I did was point and tell her to get out. She wasn't stupid because she left.

The nurse came in and told Michael and I that it could be a long time before anything would happen. Our baby was tired and getting fussy. Odd story though about our daughter. Michael and I decided that he needed to go home and let her nap and eat and they were saying good-bye she laid down on my chest and just patted me. Michael and I just looked at each other but I had to just tear up because she was so sweet and loving. Michael and I kissed each other and they left.

The next part of this story is not something I will add in this book because it doesn't really fit but I experienced something life changing. I will say though that I went to the bathroom and caught one of my boys in my hands. All I could do is look at this tiny little boy in my hands. I called for the nurse and they helped me to the bed. I told them to call Michael and let him know what was going on. I will say that we lived 30 minutes from the hospital and that is if there was not a lot of traffic. Michael made it in 15 during rush hour with our daughter.

When he walked in I had already lost them and they were trying to get the placenta out. What Michael saw was a bunch of scalpels and stuff being used on me to get the placenta out. Now I will add that up to this point I had not been given anything not even an aspirin. Michael walked over handed the baby to the nurse and told the Doctor to stop because I was climbing the walls in pain. He walked over and took my hand and he asked if I wanted anything and I told him a joint. I don't remember saying this actually after

I lost them it all became a blur because of the pain. I was screaming loudly and asking Michael to make them stop and with a very cold look he told the doctor to stop and to put her under if they needed to do that.

The next thing I knew I was waking up in recovery. Michael walked in to check on me. He told me that they let him hold his sons. He asked me if I wanted to hold them and I told him no. I asked where our little girl was and he told me with the nurse. He told me that they were going to admit me overnight. The next day when Michael came to pick me up he said he could hear me whaling as he got off the elevator. His night was not any better because he had to go home and take care of our children with no time to grieve.

Loosing children is the hardest thing any parent can go through. If you have never lost children you cannot understand the heart ache. The emptiness of it all is so overwhelming. You cry so much and so hard that there is no sound or tears. It is a pain I would never wish on anyone. My husband was my rock. He took it all on without any concern for the horrors he was going through. He sheltered me from the world. He took care of all the details. He shut out all of his feelings to take care of me and our kids. Without my husband I don't know what would have happened. I feel bad that I put all the responsibility and made him carry all the weight. I just could not handle it. My mind was empty. People say I'm sorry for your loss but every time you hear that you just want them to disappear because they have no clue what sorrow is. I know it is all they can say to you but we would rather hear and feel nothing. There is nothing you can say or do that will pull the world back together.

This took its toll on both of us. It changed both of us to the core. The loss of my twins brought me to God in a wonderful way, which in turn brought my girls to God also. That is the only benefit that the loss of my twins had on our family. The rest of it was misery. I went into a deep state of depression. I had good days but most of the time I was just going through the motions.

During this time Michael was lost. He needed me but I wasn't there. He understood why but he wanted me to be there for him. It tore his heart apart watching me go through this because I was not good for him or our children. After about 6 months he began to wonder if it wouldn't be better to take the kids and leave allowing me to work through things. Leaving though was not something he wanted for him or the kids and he didn't really want to do that to me. So he began talking to me in a way that finally brought me back to where I needed to be. I made it with some tough love that Michael knew I needed only to get slapped again 2 years to the day after losing the boys I lost another baby.

I need to say throughout our marriage he has always been there for me and I have always been there for him. It brings a smile to my face when I think about that. Even after all these years I still smile and giggle a bit when I think about him. I still love his smell. I know that we will stand the test of time because we love each other to the depths of eternity. Ok I'm done being mushy so back to my story.

We are a work in progress but we are in it for the long run. After everything we have been through it lets us know what we mean to each other and what we would do for each other. Some of you reading this book are going to think that your problems are something that cannot be worked out because you think they are too hard. Well I'm here to tell you that if you were meant to be together nothing should tear you apart.

The things I just told you didn't even shake our marriage. So when I hear people say "This is to hard… He doesn't understand me….. She never does anything I want to do." I wonder are you talking about things. Are you really expressing your feelings or are you just making a blanket statement like 'he is a butt' or 'she is a witch' but not explaining why you think that. They can't fix or understand what they are or are not doing unless you explain what you mean by those blanket statements.

On top of all those troubles we have been homeless, broke, jobless, and struggling to keep our head above water. I think that life struggles helps bond people together in a way that daily life cannot. I feel sad for this coming generation that looks at relationships as not forever but as a right now. It seems that when life gets hard they run. They are only in it for themselves without the consideration of the one they are with. With the world being a self-gratifying world…forever means…until it gets hard.

I know we have lasted all this time because of communication. We have always talked about everything, even when one of us doesn't want to. Trust me there have been conversations over the years that have not been easy for us but we still try because that is what matters. We care enough to make the effort to make things work even when it is hard.

Now you're probably wondering why I wrote this book. Well, it's the "Glitch". That is what our ongoing problems are that we work through.

That is why I'm writing this. A secret some people will keep because it can wreck a happy home faster than anything. The secret people will keep from everyone... friends and family... co-workers and for good reason. The actions and the looks from others sometimes can be too much. I will admit that my situation is an odd one and I will say that most people will not have all the topics as mine but the bottom line ends up the same. When you find your soul mate there is always a way to work out anything.

The only quality my husband has that, at given points, I would like to change is his "Glitch". Oddly enough it has brought some wonderful adventures and can in the abstract be a wonderful thing but it can cause some real problems. Actually the problems only come when things are not handled in the best way by Michael.

I know I am the only woman in his life, besides our girls, and I will always be the only women. I know that without a doubt he will love me forever. I know that I am his Hera and he is my Zeus. I am perfectly fine with that. Now for the Glitch...my husband is bi., which means he is attracted to men and women.

The judgmental thoughts in your head right now are the reasons you would never know if you are one of the women whose husbands are keeping this secret from because they feel you cannot be trusted with this information. This is why they step out and you will never know.

CHAPTER 5

Michael and I are meant to be together. Through all the ups and downs of our life we have been there for each other. We laugh together, talk together, play together, we have each other's backs, we love, cry, laugh, this is our marriage. We have a very special relationship where we talk about everything and share everything. Most people do not have this and I am not sure why. I love the fact that my husband is my best friend that I can share everything with. The glitch takes up some time in our marriage but when the glitch is not a factor we have a solid all-consuming love affair that would rival the world's greatest love stories. We talked about what to name the book and figured because if you ask most gay people they would not choose to be gay. All the ridicule, teasing, the hatred shoved at them all the time, the lack of equality who would ever choose to be gay...so we call it a glitch.

In the beginning of our life together he wasn't acting on any of his feelings. He thought that it was a phase and that it would just pass or that the internet and shower alone time would be enough. I had suspicions of things but knew nothing of what was going on with him. I didn't waste much time on the suspicions. Let me explain a bit further by starting when we first met.

I knew there was something different about my husband when we first met not in his actions but a feeling. The way he decorated his house was very nice. Now some of you are rolling your eyes but I had never really had a lot of experience with anyone like him. I had a gay friend in my wild days but he was the typical limp wristed, over the top, soft acting, and overtly gay type of person. Now don't get me wrong he was an amazing friend and a lot of fun but that is all I had ever known about gay people. The gay lifestyle that you see on T.V. and then my friend were my only examples of the gay scene. For another thing why is it always the drastic people that get all the national attention? This makes everyone believe that the entire group acts that way. For example, you always have the crazy thinking Christians who let stupidity spew from their mouths. Not once do they ever think that if Jesus actually acted that way He would have had no followers. Whatever their reason ... that is all you see or read about. Just like gay people...they are all the crazy acting ones. Actually I thought that was how they all acted because I had never seen or been around any other type...my eyes were about to be wide open.

I never did pry and I was never judgmental when odd things happened. When he showed me magazines he claimed he had found. Or the odd look he would get on his face sometimes when an attractive man was on T.V. One day sitting at the kitchen table he asked me an odd question. He asked what I wouldn't do sexually. Without really thinking I told him dead people and animals. Yea, I'm a bit of a freak...I know. He liked that answer because it told him I was not closed minded. I have always been an open type of person...what you see is what you get and if you don't like it move on no skin off my teeth. I personally think we all have a bit of freak deep down it just depends on how comfortable we are with ourselves and those around us if the truth comes out.

Michael has always put me and our children first. That is why I love him and that is why I stay and allow him to experience his glitch. You know it is better to tell you through the rest of the book only this time I will include the glitch. Now I understand the attraction to men because I am attracted to men and for the most part he likes them for the same reason. Who doesn't like a nice chest, great eyes, nice butt, and we cannot forget that predatory look men get when they are on the prowl. Now my husband doesn't care about the eyes but the whole package has to look nice and put together well...He likes men. Not some watered down version but men.

So trust me I understand why men are attractive. Since I have been with my fair share of men I can honestly ask...who doesn't like being rode hard and put away wet. If you are going to do a job I want to know you have been there at least for a couple of days. That is my opinion though.

Plus men have an outie and an inny. Now something I don't get is Lesbians. Maybe because I look at the world more like a male … I don't know. I am not a touchy feely type of person so during sex I do not need to cuddle I want hard core sex. My relationship is the same way. I do not need to be told every day what a wonderful person or how happy you are that you met me. I get that because of your actions and the look you have in your eyes…I do not need to be told. From my limited knowledge of lesbians they are more connected on an emotional level. I like hard core penetration.

Toys are nice, don't get me wrong, we have a few ourselves but that is not the same as a human's warm touch. I knew plenty of guys that would not have cared being used as a toy. I am not an emotional person so men are more appealing to me because they are not emotional. I figure that is why I have always been closer to men than women. I understand the logic of a man.

Yes I do have emotions but not in a sappy way. Unfortunately, the way most people see women. Although trust me I have days not many but a few Michael and I call my girl days but anyway I see lesbians more into an emotional connection. That is why they form their bond. While I am on the subject I will add this I also don't understand if you're attracted to women then why do you not go after one that acts and looks like a woman. This goes for men too if you're attracted to a man then go after one that acts like a man. A lot of gay men that I have talked to do not understand these things either so I guess I am not alone.

Women look for other things in men but in the gay world most, maybe not all, they are after sex. Women are too but most women want to be wined and dined before putting out. A fact I never really understood. My thoughts were, why waste my time in getting to know someone if they suck in bed. Sex is part of a relationship. It is not the only part but it is what keeps couples interested in each other on an intimate level. Later on it is a way to connect. Sex is always better with someone you know and trust. They know your secret desires and there for the sex is better. Michael knows what I like and I know what he likes so there for neither one of us are ever disappointed.

One fact I think that is over looked in the gay world or the way we look at gay men is their openness about sex. At first I thought they were just perverts but now I understand a bit better why sex is a big part of their conversation. So let's say a gay man is out at a bar and sees someone they are

36

attracted to. Unless this man is verse, which means he likes to be the top or bottom, he needs to know if they will work together. Two tops or two bottoms really do not work. So I understand a bit better not to mention what they like in bed. These thoughts are just my observations I have never really asked so this is just what I think.

Maybe I will write another book and dive into that subject but as for right now I will stick to what I know and that is Michael and I. We had been together several years before he started visiting web sites. He did not know a lot about computers and sucked at typing but he got by. One night when he came to bed he asked me what it meant when a bunch of little windows just started to pop up on the screen. At this point there was nothing I could do because the damage was already done.

After some time Michael met someone online that he wanted to hook up with. I didn't have a problem with it because to be honest I find two nice looking guys together having sex kind of hot. It took me back to one of the parties I went to when I was young. I was tired of dealing with people so I had gone off to find a quiet place upstairs in one of the bedrooms to get high by myself. I sat down in a big chair in the corner of the dimly lit room. As I lit the joint I was going to smoke I noticed two men on the bed. One of them had shoulder length wavy black hair, a ripped tan body and the bluest eyes I had ever seen. The other one had shorter dirty blonde hair built more like a very toned surfer. They looked at me for a second and then right before my eyes they began to create live porn for me. It was mesmerizing. It wasn't soft and loving it was rough and hard. As I smoked my joint I began to play with myself. It was hot to watch. Image two of the most attractive men you have ever seen fighting for dominance. You know one punching the other in the chest followed by a growl. Grabbing each other's neck and forcing the head down on the bed. It was as if the one was trying to fuck the other so hard they would go through the bed. It took my breath away. I felt warm and moist. They asked if I wanted to join all I said was continue. When I got off I walked over to them and handed them a joint and said enjoy I know I did. To this day I get horny every time I think of that. Anyway back to what I was saying.

So I said ok about him going to meet this guy. I stayed at the house with the girls and played outside. The only thing I told him was he better brush his teeth before he kissed me when he got home. When he got back he said it was ok. I asked him what he meant and he just explained that it was not what he thought it would be and that he probably was not going to pursue it anymore. That was up to him but I was honored that he felt comfortable with us to have even brought it up to me.

That evening, though, started about 6 months of hell with the end result being we lost the twins. We both changed due to that situation. I drew closer to God and he didn't. It is not that he lost his faith he just decided to not live the life he had been living but to live more for himself. After that things got hard for both of us. Like I said I went through a year of being in a deep hole with no light and he was wondering if the old me would ever return. Sure there were some good days but it was hard for me because of all the changes.

One night I got on the internet to chat with some people and found a conversation he was having with a guy where he told the guy to meet him at work. He had told me he was done with it all. The old me would not have thought anything about it but the transformation I went through because of the loss of our boys changed things. We had been walking the same path and I had told him several times that I was glad that he was not interested in that stuff anymore and he said he agreed. However, it was a lie.

He had been fighting his feelings about the subject for a long time and was tired of waiting for the right time to talk to me. He knew I was going through a rough time after losing the twins. He was right I wasn't ready. I had found God which brought me such joy. A path he had followed for a long time. We talked about his feelings and how they were wrong to have so when he said he was done we were walking the same path.

Trying to save unneeded issues between us because of everything going on he just did it. No he should have never lied because we talk about everything. If he was having a problem or was thinking something he should have shared those feelings with me. We teach our kids to say what you mean well this goes for adults as well. He knew how important my new journey was and did not want to interfere with that. For that I thank him. The lies though, well I found out and yes the issues started.

First problem was I don't like to be lied to whether or not I understand why it was done it is extremely disrespectful. To me this is the equivalent of being called stupid. Second problem was he was the only one working and in my opinion he disregarded the fact. If he would have gotten caught it would have made us and our kids homeless for sex. Sex with some random person he had never met and didn't know anything about. The last problem was just that he didn't know him. The guy could have showed up and killed him. Shown up with friends and beat him so that he couldn't walk. They could have gotten his information which would have brought them back to the house where the girls and I could have been hurt or killed all over sex.

Michael didn't know or think about any of that. Last thing that I need to point out was the fact it would be cheating. The guy never showed up so we will never know what would have happened. That still didn't fix the fact he set it up in the first place. I talked to him before he went to work and he said nothing would happen and he said nothing did. At this point I had no reason not to believe him besides how would I know anyway one way or another.

I'll talk about the glitch for a minute. I can't fully understand the glitch because I don't have the glitch. All I can say that I understand is why men are attractive. I know that sex can be a powerful driving factor in behavior. I know it affects my behavior because if I don't get it I can be a real bitch. Some can control it others cannot and do horrible things to people which lands them in jail and that to me is the easy way out. Then there are those who just get wrapped up in the want and will sometimes put themselves in harm's way without thinking about it.

I know what it is like being in heat. It's like an itch you can't scratch. The itch is so bad that it drives you crazy. You so want it to stop that you are willing to do anything for it to stop even use glass, which you know will hurt you. It is all you can think about; getting off. It consumes every thought. Your body aches you want it so bad. You are ready for a football team to just tag team you. This is called going into heat. It is not an excuse but something I understand because I have been there.

I know the feelings are different when Michael wants another male. It is hard to put in words though because I don't fully understand it. I figure it is because I don't have those feeling. I know what type of sex Michael likes to have though. Michael likes the hard core stuff you know the stuff I describe earlier. I would think because men are not made for that hole to be used that way it wouldn't feel good but I guess no pain no gain.

I know that some people say that if it wasn't supposed to feel good then the prostate wouldn't be located where it is. I know that people say massaging the prostate is supposed to make a man get off but everything I have read it is just in an area of the body close to the penis because it makes fluid for sperm so it would have to be in that area. So because it is part of the reproductive system it would feel good. I am not a doctor or a gay male so who knows.

So now back to the story ... where was I ... oh yea the secret meeting Michael set up for his work. So this guy that he never did anything with and who never showed up lead to a long talk about what Michael needed. How could we work this out between us so that we both could be happy? We had both gone through changes but we loved each other and did not want to give up on us. He didn't want me to compromise my walk and I didn't want him to be ½ a person.

We sat together and he explained how he tried to stop the feelings. He told me that feeling that way bothered him and he hated it but couldn't fix it. He was sorry for lying to me and didn't want to lie anymore. This was an avenue he needed to look into. He hoped I would stay with him till he figured things out because he loved me and the kids and our life together. He wanted me to understand he couldn't fix it but it wouldn't change the way he felt about me in any way. We came to an understanding, that night, that I would try and give it a shot. I wouldn't condone his behavior but I wasn't the one doing it. Something I had learned in my walk so far with God is everyone's walk is their own. Michael needed to walk his own walk.

During this conversation he told me that a guy had called him while he was working and told him that he was interested in him but that if Michael wasn't then he was sorry. Michael had never really experienced this type of behavior with anyone in the "real" world. When it came to dealing with someone hitting on him in that way, a man, it was a new thing for him. He had never seen him so he didn't know what to expect. Here was someone who saw him in the real world, his straight world. He was very nervous because when the guy first asked him he told the guy no and that he was straight. During the conversation he told him he was actually bi. As the conversation went on Michael got his number.

Funny, looking back that meant that he already had his number before I said yes. I wonder what would have happened if I had said no. He would have just lied again I'm sure. At the time though I wanted to help my husband and be supportive I loved him and felt bad for him. He was dealing with something that was new for him and I did not want to complicate things for him.

He went a few times to hang out with the guy before they hooked up. I was not excited about it but I figured, at the time, to let him get it out of his system. Once it was it would be over and I wouldn't have to worry about it anymore. At this point in our relationship I didn't understand the dynamics of being bi. To be completely honest after all these years I still don't fully understand. There are always new and odd things popping up that we deal with.

I have asked my husband and he says it is the same type of attraction that he feels for a woman sexually not emotionally. When you see an attractive body you become aroused but for him it does not matter what sex they are he can find them sexually arousing. Some men watch themselves beat off in a mirror and they are turned on by it. Just like, for example, the guy at the gym checking themselves out in the mirror. You can tell the ones making sure their form is right and the ones that look like they are turning themselves on. I would say they have a bit of bi in them because they can be turned on by a male.

Maybe it is because sex between 2 people of the same sex is taboo and that makes it kinky. Michael says maybe that is why it is such a turn on. When you give up control, even if it is slight, that can be a turn on. Men who are always the top or in charge, such as a very demanding job in their everyday life, to become a bottom gives up "control". Which I can understand because men are always in control it would be nice to be in control sometimes.

Controlling those feelings of being bi or gay are complex. You cannot sum up what it is like to be bi in just a few sentences to understand it. I was afraid it was something that was here to stay. I had hoped that the day would come where it would all be over and I wouldn't have to worry about it anymore. Maybe by letting him be with this guy would show him that it wasn't what he wanted and it would be over. These feelings would be put in the past and we could go back to where we were.

After he got home from hooking up with him he told me it wasn't like it was in porn and he was done. Michael was still new at the whole bi thing so he didn't fully understand everything either. As far as hooking up he felt he was done because it was not fulfilling. For him how could you be attracted to something that didn't live up to expectations? He felt porn and beating off with a toy would be enough. It was painful and made no since to Michael. Why would he be with someone when it was uncomfortable and was not fun when he knew he could take the toy we had which was bigger and felt good? Why put yourself through that? Unfortunately this didn't fix the problem forever and he began looking again to fix the problem.

We talked about making a big change in our lives by buying a house. Michael bought me a beautiful dog, and English Mastiff. I loved my puppy she was very unique she would sit in the window when we left and wait for us and when we would come home her teeth would chatter. If you don't know what an English Mastiff is they get to be about 250 pounds. They think they weigh 10 pounds and are just as small. They make wonderful family dogs.

So the house we were looking at was great. The house had a nice big back yard for our kids to play in. The basement had an apartment in part of it and we figured that would come in handy either to rent it out or for one of our parents to use when they got older. The bedrooms were nice size and it had 3 full bathrooms. It was perfect. The seller backed out leaving us nowhere to go so the girls and I stayed with his mother for a short time.

I tried my best to get along with his mom I really did. I worked my butt off trying to do things for her because she was old and not in really good shape. I fixed the foundation on her driveway and shed. Poured concrete to fix her walk way. I cleaned up her side yard that was over grown and had all these big rocks imbedded in the ground. I used all the big rocks and made her a rock garden. I bought all our food that we ate and even some for them. I did all these things because she was letting us stay with her. I tried to do dishes and cook but she wouldn't let me. She would get mad if I ran the sweeper. Now if I didn't do all those things she would complain that I never did anything and was taking advantage of her. I knew this because that is what she said about her daughter. Every time she tried to run the sweeper or do her own laundry Michael's mom would stop her and then complain to me that her daughter was lazy and never did anything. She is one of the oddest women I have ever met. Her logic is so off.

One example was when our oldest daughter thought she would be nice and make her grandmother some coffee. She walked into the living room all excited and handed her a cup of coffee and told her she had made it herself. When our oldest went back into the kitchen she heard her grandmother say … Great now I bet they expect me to take them into town to buy water she knows her mom cannot drink our water. When my daughter told me what she had overheard I packed a big lunch and took the girls to walk a mile to buy water so she wouldn't have to.

We had a ball that day walking to the store. We took our time because we had nothing else to do. One of the things we did was stop at an old cemetery. I always liked reading the old head stones. This was something my Grandma got me started doing. It was exciting when we saw a deer up close and personal. It walked almost up to us where we could have touched it. We played games like I Spy while we walked. I really had a great day with my girls.

A lady had passed us twice on our way to the store. The third time she stopped and told me and the girls to get in she would take us the little bit we had left and back home. We had already been gone about 5 hours. The girls and I thanked her for her kindness and the ride. When she dropped us off all his mother said was…great what will everyone think of me letting you walk all that way. You are kidding right…yup she is nuts.

The final straw though came one morning when my daughter went in to get the phone for me so I didn't have to take the baby out of the room. The baby seemed to get on their nerves so I kept her back in the room a lot with me. Every morning I would call Michael and he would talk to the girls and I for a little bit while he was at work. This would be really the only time I would get to talk to him and him to us. My daughter came back empty handed and said we were not going to be able to use the phone anymore. Again we got up and left.

There was a little church up the road a short way and this is where we spent most of our time. I would pack a lunch and the girls and I would go up there and play. They had a small playground with swings and a slide. We went to the church almost every day. I asked the preacher if I could call my husband. I told Michael what was going on and told him I didn't want to be there anymore and neither did the girls. I knew we had to stay but he told me he would work on it.

The girls and I were playing on the playground when I saw Michael pull up. I started crying and so did our youngest. We all ran over to hug him. We walked inside the church to talk. He told me that he couldn't leave his babies there anymore and kissed me. He told me he asked our friend if we could all stay there just until we found a place and she had said yes. So we all drove down to his moms packed our stuff out of the one room we all had to share and left. I and the kids were never so happy to leave a place in our life.

We found a place after about a week. It was nice and in town. It was a two story two bedroom duplex with a garage and I loved it. I would have loved anything being away from his mother. My oldest agreed with me. His mom never really acted like a grandmother to our oldest and actually it was that behavior that kept us from talking to her for over a year for the second time during our relationship.

When we moved back in together I found pictures on his phone. I asked him about them because as far as I knew he was done. He wasn't. We had another conversation where he told me again that he tried but it was something that he couldn't control. He wanted to try and meet up with someone again. I didn't understand why he had to lie to me. I didn't understand why he couldn't just come to me and tell me. We had been through so much and by now he should trust me because all the secrets were only causing us harm. I felt if I had to find out myself then he was lying and keeping secrets from me.

All the bullshit that I had already gone through with Michael about this subject was hard enough without finding out things myself. I was tired of him being distant ever time this subject reared its ugly head. I wanted my husband back so I asked him if he could let me wrap my head around the idea before he did anything and he agreed. I needed to trust him again which was not an easy thing since it seemed he lied all the time about it. He understood my position because of all the lies but how could I trust someone to step out of the marriage and believe it was all just sex.

He began to visit sites and chat with people. There was only one thing that I asked from him was that he didn't tell anyone where he was or show his face on any of the sites. I even took pictures for him to put on the site and to send to people that he was talking to. I knew all his passwords to all the sites he was on. I didn't want my husband's picture or address up on any of these sights because of our daughter. Over the years I have had to make him change it because he doesn't listen. For her safety at school because kids are cruel I don't want someone finding out. Over the years it has been an ongoing battle with him.

Oh a quick word of warning to women who find this out about their husbands...they all lie on these sites to make themselves look better or to excite the person they are talking to. They could be sitting watching T.V. and say they are having some wild escapade with the neighbor. Read everything with a grain of salt and think back you will begin to see a pattern arise and you will be able to pull out the bullshit stuff. I know that you will want to read it but really just let it go. That doesn't mean don't look to make sure he is not into things you cannot handle but reading the conversations will lead you down a path you will not like.

I have found over the years it is best not to read this because all it will do is drive you deeper into the hole you are already in. I am not sure why men lie to everyone about what they are not really doing because if they thought about it then they would realize that they are probable being lied to also. Oh well that's on them.

During this time Michael met a guy on line that wanted him to do porn. After talking to this guy online, thru emails and on the phone I agreed to help. I took pictures of him so the guy could show other people. They still chat to this day but the porn adventure never happened. The guy was very interested in our situation and asked a lot of questions. He told Michael that network companies were interested in something like this and he was working on a script for it but had no idea about what was going to happen. Michael told me back then that I should write about our life. At the time I was still trying to get my head around it all. I didn't want to write a book I really wanted it to all stop.

It was also around this point that he started doing massages. We were broke and needed money. Michael learned how to do a type of massage through his marital art training. He figured it was a way to make quick money. I figured...what harm could it do. I was not keen with the idea of him giving women massages. He and I agreed men only. This killed a few birds with one stone. He could kind of be in the gay world without being in the gay world which would fix what I thought he needed and make some money.

When my husband first got into the "massage" thing he ran into the upper class society of the gay world. The ones that think they are better than everyone else to the outside world. The ones that look down at us poor people...you know the big business types, doctors and lawyers. In this type of environment they are another type of creature all together. What I mean by another type of creature is just that they all have issues and insecurities too. They just hide theirs better. Actually some of them have way more issues than what I thought they would have. All the ones that hired him have busy lives who don't like to admit that they hire someone for companionship. I am not sure why I thought this because straight men have been doing this since the beginning of time.

Michael was not very busy at first but then it really picked up. He was going out almost all the time. I asked a few times after business picked up if he was doing anything with them and he said no except maybe a bit of groping but that was it.

After some time had gone by he said that he would like to meet this guy he was talking to on line for coffee and I agreed. There was no harm in just meeting someone for coffee. Michael lived in a house full of women with really no male friends. Nothing ever came of it because he wasn't Michaels' type plus this guy wanted to leave his wife and Michael wanted no part of that.

The next guy that he asked to hang out with started out as a client. Michael told me that he was an interesting guy and wanted to get to know him better. He set up a time when they could hang out. As he left I had my doubts about nothing happening. Still to this day all I have is his word. Michael said he was very nice to look at and had a great body. They went to the bar across from his apartment and hung out. The time they "hung out", though, he told me nothing happened. This didn't last long and Michael moved on.

Around this time our relationship became strained again. He was quiet and sex had dropped off. He and I would have conversations about him taking care of himself all the time when I was willing and ready anytime. He would also act angry towards me. Every little thing would become an argument. He spent a lot of time on the computer and by himself which took its toll on us. I began to look at it all and realized that he seemed to want an easy way out of the situation. I told him that if he wanted out he was going to have to leave I wasn't. I had put to much effort into our relationship and we had been through too much just to let it all go.

Men have their pride issues...I get that. I know that they are the ones who are supposed to take care of the family so I understood losing his job bothered him. It caused money problems but it seemed more than that. He was angry and wouldn't talk to me. He would tell me he was going out to look for a job and be gone most of the day. I found out later that he did go and look for a job but then he would also go and sit at the mall.

One time he went to an adult arcade. Now for those of you who do not know what an adult arcade, which I was one of them, I will explain. This means in the back there are booths about the size of a changing room with a TV in it. You put in your money and then you can choose what kind of porn you want to watch. The doors don't have locks on them and some guys will leave the door cracked to be watched or for someone to join them. Some guys will tap their foot to let others know of an invite. Most guys that go there are on the down low because they don't get on line or go to the clubs so this is their only form of release.

I was working at a pizza shop at this time. I was outside on one of my breaks having a cigarette when a man rode up on his bike and stopped right in front of me. He took his helmet off and smiled at me. We started up a conversation. With a nice smile he told me I should take a ride with him to the beach. The bike and the beach are my Achilles heel. I'm sorry to say but for a second I was actually thinking about it. After a bit of flirting I smiled, told him to have a nice ride and walked away.

I cannot say it wasn't tempting for a moment. I needed sex and attention which I was not getting at home. All the things that ran through my mind in those few minutes were things I really wanted from my husband. I really wanted my husband to be my mystery man who rode up on a bike. I wanted to be whisked away to have dirty sex in some public places. I wanted us to get drunk and pass out on the beach. I wanted my husband. I missed him.

I missed our long talks about nothing, our closeness. He would press his lips on the back of my neck and in a very deep sexy voice tell me that he loved me or even ask what was for dinner. I know it doesn't sound like much but I loved that. I missed my husband. I wanted to be as close as we were. I wanted to believe in him again and trust him. Writing this brings back those memories. I'm glad we made it through those times and more but at the time I felt so lost and empty.

Michael came to me with an idea about doing web cam. At first I really didn't know what to think or even what it really was. He explained it to me and told me there wasn't much time spent on the computer so I agreed.

The short amount of time he spent on the computer the paycheck was nice. That was short lived though. It wasn't that it was a hard job… play on words ha-ha…but it is hard to do anything with a little girl knocking on the door wanting to see her daddy. He is a good dad because he would get off the web cam and spend time with the family.

One day I was cleaning the living room and found, what I thought, was the vacuum cleaner belt. I was mad because I thought the vacuum was broke. I took off the bottom and saw that it wasn't. Not thinking anything of it I laid it on the entertainment center and finished cleaning. Michael came home and I asked him why he got it out. Well, it wasn't so funny after that because it was actually a cock ring that he had left in the living room. He thinks it is still funny.… I don't but whatever. On a ha-ha got you back kind of thing, he lost that cock ring when he got arrested on a traffic violation. He was worried they would search him so he tossed it in the holding cell back by the toilet.

Now I just realized that you may not know what a cock ring is. To put it nicely it goes around the base of his twig and berries. This is supposed to make their erection harder and make it last longer. It makes their package stand out nicely. It is used for other things but I think you get the idea.

He met a guy on Craigslist who was doing club promoting and needed an assistant to help him run a show he was hired to run. Michael talked to him and got the job. I was very scared because where as I know my husband can take care of himself there is always someone bigger and bader than you are. I always get nervous when he leaves to meet anyone off the internet. That night he went out to help him with the show. It was a long night for me.

He was gone till almost 3 in the morning. I have never really been able to sleep if he is gone. I am not sure why I enjoy the bed all to myself but I just cannot sleep well when anyone is gone from the house. So I sat up and waited to find out all the things that went on at the event. It was a very nice event he had a lot of fun. It had lots of music and a fashion show of sorts. Michael said it was a very interesting and well planned event. We sat up for a while talking about all the stuff that happened that night. He said his feet hurt almost the whole time but he loved it.

CHAPTER 6

Now this is where the story takes a twist. Yes, I know what you're thinking. There have already been enough crazy curves but this next one really started the fun part of it all. Michael came home after one of his clients with an interesting story. He told me that the guy he had just done a massage for books guys to dance at clubs and wanted him to be one of his dancers. Sounds fun ... well neither of us really understood that.

We both figured you dance around in jeans and no shirt or something. Well that wasn't the case. The client wanted him to dance in his underwear. Now don't get me wrong Michael is a great dancer. Michael loves to dance. Sad thing is he is not very outgoing. He is actually pretty reserved.

So to be honest we didn't really understand what that was but Michael was excited but nervous. Well scared might be a better word. Michael is not a very outgoing person. He is actually very reserved. He loves to dance and is very good at it. He knows he is very good at it but still to put yourself out there like that was not his style. So when he said he was going to do it I was a bit thrown.

I remember the first night he left. I told him he looked great and tried my best to help the anxieties. He asked several times about his hair and if he looked good. To me Michael always looked good but I knew what he meant. I made sure there was no hair sticking up and that his clothes looked good. I was nervous for him but I smiled, gave him a kiss and told him to have fun. I also told him if he didn't like it he should at least try it because dancing was something he loved to do. He gave me a big hug and kiss before he left and we said we would talk when he got home.

We did talk that night but Michael needed a lot of liquid courage to dance so the majority of the conversation was the next day. I waited up for him and fixed him something to eat because he was starving. I figured that he would be since he didn't eat before he left. That night he said that everyone was excited to see him and let him know they were happy he was there. I didn't find out till I started going out on how that community showed their happiness.

Michael opted to leave some of the story parts out. I figured it was like being a stripper. You can watch them dance but you are not to touch them. I never understood why people would ever be into that because why do I want to pay for something I cannot touch. Little did I know this is not the case when you dance at a gay bar. Touching is something they look forward to and trust me they do. Well, all these curves will make good stories for when we are sitting on our porch when we are old.

Michael was still doing clients and now he was dancing sometimes on the weekend. At first I never really went with him. I enjoyed the stories he told me when he would come home. We would sit up and laugh about all the weird things that he would tell me about. Now I know what you're thinking, after all the lies how can I just believe everything he is saying. To be honest I don't know I just did. I had to if we were going to make it work. Logically thinking you always want to believe the one you're with because they are not supposed to lie to you.

I guess I was hoping all the lies were behind us because that is what he told me and as a wife we should be able to believe our husbands. With me being the one that was lied to I was the one who had to start trusting again. At this part of my life I wanted to believe him. As far as I knew he wasn't lying about anything so why wouldn't I believe him. Trust had to start with me and I knew that. I needed to be the one who showed him I was ok with his life decisions even when I wasn't fully. I had stopped reading all the emails and stuff. Most of the conversations were not that interesting.

Most of them were the same conversations over and over. Oh, they used different words but honestly they were not very thought provoking. Trust me when I say none of them made me question him or his honesty. The conversations were almost like what you hear at a bar when someone is trying to pick you up. I found it funny that men use the same lame lines on other men as they do women. I thought men were so much more direct with each other, some are, but some are just as lame gay as they are straight.

We were headed down two different paths now. Michael was headed down a single man's path and I was headed down a single mom's path. Michael was spending a lot of time booking clients, talking to people and dancing. I was dealing with kids, the house, the yard, cooking and a kidney stone in my right kidney the size of a $.50 piece. I was also dealing with depression. Depression is a tricky animal. You do not know you have depression until you are so far down there is no light. It makes it hard to see life clearly and dealing with everything and depression I was blind.

I never knew depression could affect so many aspects of your life. There were days I would walk around in sweats not bothering to brush my hair or anything. I figured I wasn't going anywhere why bother. I stayed stressed out all the time over nothing really. I would ache in my joints for no reason and I would have really bad headaches. Depression is nothing to joke about but it is mind over matter for some because if you take precautions to keep yourself up and going things do get better. Unfortunately when you start on the downward spiral you don't know that is what you're doing.

After losing the kids, I had gained a lot of weight and was not happy with myself. Our relationship suffered because of it. Our sex life suffered, not that it was an everyday event when we first met before all this but now it would be months sometimes. Now let me explain a bit about me and Michael though to ya.

I am very much into sex, Michael is not but he is very sexual. What that means in a nutshell is I love the act of sex and Michael likes the thought of sex. Michael can watch porn all day and never have sex. I watch porn and all I want to do is have sex...right then. He likes turning people on and as soon as I try that I am ready to go. I would drop everything for a good time in bed but Michael likes to play around just to play around. I on the other had could have sex morning, noon, and night but Michael can go for some time without having it or pleasuring himself. If I were a guy I would be beating off probably 10 times a day. It is much easier for them so yes I have a bit of penis envy.

Also, looking back at what I looked like I wouldn't have wanted to sleep with me either. I know I wasn't the person I was and didn't know how to get back there. We had joined a gym but I just couldn't get into it. I did when he was helping me but I needed help and he tried but not the way I needed him to. One day I looked at myself in the mirror and I was done.

My outlook and where I wanted to be changed right then and there. I started losing weight and trying to pull myself out of a very deep hole I was in. I'm not where I want to be yet but I'm getting there, I have had a few setbacks but no more. I went from 550lbs and now I have about 100lbs more to lose. I still have a hard time getting in the mood and money for the gym is an issue but I know I will get there.

Michael's 1st dance gig was at a bar called Flexx. It was upstairs in this old building downtown. This area of downtown had fallen on hard times and was not very nice but the city was trying to bring it back. At the top of the steps was a small room which opened up into a larger room. It had a few seating areas in the bar but not many and the dance floor was around the boxes the boys danced on. The make-shift DJ area was close to the exterior wall of the bar. Michael told me that they danced on raised boxes in the middle of the room. Actually every time the boy's dance it is usually on raised boxed boxes or on a bar. The bar dancing does not happen very often.

The first dance gig he did was with a porn star named Trever Knight. When he came home he was full of stories. Michael's first story was about one of the dancers that danced with him that night. We will just call him Mark. I gave you a name only for this paragraph so don't worry he is not that important other than the funny thing I learned about him. Scott had a hard time getting Mark to dance unless there was a porn star. Mark would only dance if there was a porn star at the event. That was because he went home with the porn stars. I only saw him dance one time and guess what... yup it was on a night there was a porn star dancing... and yes he did go back to his hotel with him. I can't say to much he has become a small celebrity himself... although listing to all the whining he did on Facebook I wonder why.

Another story he told me about was that one of the times he went back stage a guy had a pair of his underwear in his hands smelling them. Yes you heard what I said and yes that is gross but ... to each their own I guess. The story didn't end there because as Michael tried to get his underwear back the guy pulled down his underwear and wanted to give him a blow job. I laughed because when I was watching Michael tell the story his facial expressions were priceless. The first term I ever learned was "fresh meat". Yup it means what you think it does only in that world everyone and their brother tries to get you to do things with them.

Michael noticed that the looks people had on their face made them an open book. They all wanted sex with him in one form or another. Some of the looks would keep you from walking down a dark alley with them. They were acting like peacocks strutting around making sure Michael noticed them. All their actions were intentional trying to grab his attention so he would take an interest in them. To bad in the area we are there are not to many guys Michael finds hot. They think they are hot but they are sadly mistaken. Most guys that approach Michael he wouldn't sleep with, well maybe if they paid him.

He danced a few other places when Scott would call. Michael loved to dance but there were not many gigs Scott got him at first. He was still doing clients when we lost the place we were living. We moved in with a friend of ours and stayed with her for about six months. We lived beside her for about two years and that is how we met. She was a very good friend and had three wonderful kids.

Michael told me about a fashion show and we talked to his sister who was trying to get into modeling. We took Lisa, Michael's sister, to meet with Scott about a runway show. This was the first time I had ever met Scott. He was an odd kind of person. Really stand offish to me, which I found out later it was due to the fact he didn't really like women. He had no use for them at all. Scott was a middle aged grey haired man about 5'9" and slightly on the heavy side. He never really smiled. I figured because he was gay they were happy people. Yes I know that is a stereotype but I didn't know anything yet so give me a break. I know differently now.

Michael had been dancing for Scott for about a year now and I had seen a real change in him. I still never had the opportunity to go with Michael because we had a little girl and no babysitter. The stories were still funny to listen to. Over the years I have found out little things he left out of some of his stories. On the one hand it is nice to know he is comfortable to say things and talk about them as if I knew what he was talking about. On the other hand, though, I have to wonder what he is still keeping from me. He says that he didn't tell me everything to save my feelings or because he knew it would make me mad and cause problems. There are problems with that logic ... I don't feel Michael should be doing anything that would cause problems or make me mad. Actually to his credit if I had known all the things that went on I wouldn't have been secure enough in all of it to be ok with it.

When I find out he has been dishonest by doing things that would have made me upset or things that I have asked him not to do...it pisses me off. Yes, it is in the past but it is still, in my opinion, a betrayal. He knew how I would feel and didn't care about that because he still did whatever it was. The way he explains it makes a good argument but it is still cheating and lying to someone you say you love and care about. He says that it never changed the way he felt about me or us so why cause problems where there are none. I think that is a BS way to look at things but it is easy to say things like that when things are not being done to you. I am glad though I didn't find out back then though because he was right about it causing problems.

There are moments when I wonder about what he has not told me. So you can imagine the thoughts I have. I have a very big imagination so what actually happened and what I imagine are two different things. See I picture him taking people to the back room and fucking their brains out leaving them lying on the floor in a puddle. Now I know that doesn't happen because there is not enough time for that. There are also other things that I know about now that make that a non-starter anyway but I might get into that later. I will say Michael doesn't like the smell of sex or ass so unless they were cleaned out that would never happen.

Still I wonder on some of the nights knowing what I know now and how good of a liar he is what happened. I shouldn't have to because I should not be lied to but I have been so I wonder. I know there has been a lot of groping done. The only thing I have problems with is the way I look at sex. The sex between a man and woman is all I know I didn't know any other way. I never watched gay porn so all I see is the way I know it.

This is not the way Michael has sex and it is not in his personality but even the kissing thing bothers me. After listening to the stories I wanted to see for myself. I wanted to know what really was going on. This is the beginning of me being thrust into a strange world. A world I thought I had all figured out but I was SO wrong.

CHAPTER 7

Now before I tell you about my first outing into this world let me say ... Everything you see on TV is BS. The gay world is not like that at all. Yes there are aspects of it that you do see but for the majority of it they are not like that at all. Sure they have their little quirks but so do we all. They are wonderful beautiful people who are just like everyone else except they know how to have a good time. I know that now but then I was scared and extremely nervous when I had my first look into the gay world.

Now before I go into the story of my first outing let me set the stage. Michael had been going out dancing for about a year. He had already danced at Flexx, Chris's, and Tom's Cabaret. He had already met some of the people I will talk about later, which I will put them in the book as I met them such as Allen, Scott, Mark, Jeff, Brent, Wayne, JR, Brian, Blake, Blane, Bobby and Nathan, which I absolutely love and know now but this wonderful man would travel 2 hours just to see Michael and Hunter dance which is amazing in itself and he was married with his wife and son at home...there are other people that I know now and have met but if I put everyone in here the book would be a to long to read. There were other things that happened with Michael that he kept to himself because if I had found out at the time he would have been dead. I have issues with finding things out later but it is so far in the past that it makes no sense now to be mad I just add a punch to the long list of free punches I owe him. He didn't tell me about all the fondling, grouping, grabbing, kissing even though there wasn't much of that but I would have been mad but what happened at Flexx would have been a game changer if I had found out then. Remember when I told you about

Trever Night, the porn star, I might have forgotten to mention how drunk Michael when he got home. This is thanks to the bartender which leads into the story I am about to tell you. Flex liked to change the look almost every time Michael was there. The gogo boxes were at the far end of the room with a bar beside each gogo box which made it easy for them to get drinks whether they wanted them or not. This particular bartender had been flirting with Michael every time he saw him making it perfectly clear that he wanted to be with Michael. At this time Michael was not stepping out because of my comfortability. Men when they are horny, especially when they go in heat, will take anything they can get. This guy was pressing Michael hot and heavy all night long and after Michael was done dancing he walked outside with this guy. Now the bar wasn't closed yet but the two of them took the conversation to the backseat of the car where they didn't do a lot of talking. I am sure you can paint the picture of what went on. My first time out with my husband dancing was interesting. He was hired to be a shot boy at a Cabaret in town; Tom's.

The color scheme in the bar was not anything spectacular. Walking in the front door the D.J. booth was right inside and a stage to the left. The bar was on the other side of the room. A small dance floor was just off the bar and the smoking area was just past the dance floor. It was a nice bar but nothing like what I was accustom to coming from the beach. I never went into a lesbian bar so I really had nothing to compare it to.

I was nervous but happy to show my support in his choices. He was nervous about me going that night. He was afraid someone was going to do anything to me to throw me into a panic. What he was really afraid of was me seeing someone do something to him that would give me the wrong idea or that I wouldn't understand. He just hoped the night went well.

After all of our talks I can honestly say I can support him but not his lifestyle choices. With our religious beliefs we both understand it is wrong but everyone's walk is their own. I can't judge him for his choices just like nobody can judge me for mine. Everyone looks at things differently and it is up to the individual to make their own choices. You cannot shove what they believe down everyones throat.

I will take a few minutes to say something to all those bible thumpers. Do you not understand that the more you hurt people with your words the more people will turn away and not listen to anything you have to say? The way to reach people is to show them by your behavior that your choices are worth looking into. You are not a follower of God in Heaven if all you do is call names and spew hate out of your mouth. My grandmother always said you will get more bees with honey than you will with vinegar. If you think what you're doing is helping you're wrong. If that type of behavior is what you think God in Heaven wants you to do you are wrong. One of my favorite phrases is "Everyone's Walk Is Their Own" and that would include you. Only you will answer for the things you are doing on earth to others. Sorry I get on a rant sometimes that I could go on and on…so anyway.

Anyway, I was excited about going. My first time out and I was going to have a good time with my hubby. I was happy he was including me in his other life. It's hard to love ½ a person. Feeling left out of ½ of his life. I wanted to understand I wanted to help him through this I wanted to be there with him and for him.

He took me shopping for something for me to wear. I did not have any clothes that you would call club clothes. We never went out together and every job I had there was a type of uniform so I didn't have clothes. I was heavy so I didn't have anything nice. We had fun because we made a day of it. When it came time to get ready I put on my new clothes and went out with my hubby.

Ever hear the term fish out of water. I was gasping for air. I had no idea what to expect when I walked in and it was an eye opener. Tom's was a drag bar and lesbian bar. My husband figured that out of all the bars in town this one would be the safest one for me to go to. He was nervous but this was a good starting point for me. Nothing really ever happened there and all in all it was a very mild club. Well it was a very calm bar minus the drama of the drag queens.

Let me tell you a bit about drag queens. Over the years I have experienced some good drag queens and some ratchet drag queens. Most drag queens I have met are called, by most, broke down or scary drag queens. There make-up and outfits are way over the top. Most of them just walk around lip-singing old songs. The other groups of drag queens try to look like women some take on the persona of a movie starlit but they still look, for the most part, like a woman. They just don't walk around some actually sing and they all dance. Some better than others, both of these groups you have the top of the class and bottom of the class as far as performing go.

Most of the drag queens I have met are very nice. One of the drag queens I have met is extremely nice and wonderful. She is very tall and slender with dark hair. He makes a nice looking man and woman oddly enough. Usually the men that make descent woman are odd looking men. We still have to have a "girl's" night out with lots and lots of drinking. I am glad to call her/him a friend.

I am amazed to find out what men go through to be a drag queen. Many carry scars because of it. The drag kings have scars on their chest from the tapping their boobs down so imagine the scars on the men because of drag. The other groups of drag queens are ratchet. They are the white trash of drag queens. Later I have a story and you will understand why they are called ratchet but I will leave that opinion up to you the reader but I am sure you will agree.

So now I will go back to my night out with my husband. As the bar began to fill up with people I realized I was soooo in the minority. Not as far as there were a lot of women but I was probably the only straight person in the bar. I had never been to a gay bar before so as people started coming in and behaving in a way that let me know I was not in Kansas anymore I began to feel more uncomfortable. I have to admit I was a bit scared. I was used to being the one that was important. In this world I was the outsider looking in. Michael was half in this world and I wanted to support him.

I found a quit bar stool to sit on and just watch. Right away I realized that the people in the bar were very friendly. They were not a bit scary they were just normal people just like everyone else trying to make their way in the world. I had lots of people walk up and just start talking which is not something I was used to. In a straight club everyone keeps to themselves unless they are trying to hook up. Nobody that night was trying to pick me up they were there to have a good time. It was refreshing.

Anyway I sat at the bar and just enjoyed a drink and talking to people who walked up to me. Michael came up and told me that a friend of his was there named Jeff, affectionately known as Mr. Glass. I was looking forward to meeting him because I had heard so much about him. Michael said he would send him over the next time he saw him. Anyway I was sitting there drinking my drink, watching my husband, and minding my own business when this man came up and began humping my leg while talking to me.

Talk about being thrown off your game I was hanging off a cliff by a blade of grass.

Michael came up to me and I told him what had just happened to me as I looked around the bar to show him the guy. Michael said oh there is Jeff and pointed at the guy I was talking about. Michael called him over and he told me it was nice to meet me and gave me a big hug and kiss on the cheek. Mr. Glass was so drunk but I loved his laugh and personality. He is so full of life. Mr. Glass called over his boyfriend Brent and I instantly felt a connection to both of them. Mr. Glass is a short little bomb shell with grey in his blondish brown hair and thin build. He must have a hollow leg because he can drink his weight in liquor. Brent has salt and pepper hair and just slightly heavier than Mr. Glass. Both of them are shorter than me which I find to be soooo cute.

They stood and talked to me for a bit and helped me feel not so out of place. I will always love them for that. Actually I went out several times with them and they always made me feel welcome. You know how someone will give you a hug to be nice. Well that is not the case here. They hugged me like we had been friends for years with all the warmth and kindness one can show to another person. I love both of them very much.

Michael told me that he and the other shot boy were not making very much money. Just so you know what a shot boy is I will explain. It is where you walk around the bar in your underwear and try to sell people shots. You charge $2.00 for a shot and the bar keeps a dollar and you keep the rest. So if someone gave them a $5 then the bar still only got a dollar and Michael would keep the rest. Most people will tip you like a bar tender though so if it is a good tasting shot you can make some good money.

This night, however, the bar decided to put some nasty tasting whatever it was drink in the shot that nobody wanted. They tried for a little bit but nobody wanted them because it took them forever to sell the first tray. Michael went up to the bar and asked if they could have something else. Since the bar was taking their sweet time in making more nasty shot or something else, and they were just standing around, they were asked to be part of the drag queen's act and explained to me what they were going to be doing.

The drag queens got a wild hair and wanted them for her act. She was trying to impersonate Lady GaGa by doing Poker Face. In my opinion you cannot mess up a song you're not singing. I was wrong because the visual was not that good. So anyway, I will let you decide what type of drag queen this one is after you read more about him later on.

She was going to be making her entrance right there where I was sitting so I decided to move. The show started and I watched them help her off the bar and to the stage. During the song the main drag queen made a big deal about how hot it would be to see the shot boys kiss. She pretty much shoved their heads together. The next few moments went in slow motion. I saw her push their heads together. Just as they started to kiss I turned my head and took a drink. I didn't want to see my husband kiss another man. It was ok though because when I turned around it was over. The look on my husbands' face was one of panic and fear. His worst nightmare was coming true. 1st he was scared I wouldn't understand that he didn't want that to happen and the scene that I might cause and the effects at home. 2nd he defiantly didn't want his first encounter in the gay world on stage and in-front of his wife.

I knew why it happened. I knew it was not his choice. I understood it was just part of the show. So, for me, I was fine. I was outside smoking when Michael walked up to me and started to apologize but I told him before he could finish that I was ok and understood. I loved him and I knew he would have never thrown anything in my face especially on my first night out. He has put me in some very uncomfortable situations but never with the intent of hurting me.

I went to another bar with him called Chris's. Chris's is a 2 story bar that sits on the corner of a very odd corner. There is a stop light in the middle of the intersection that can stop about 2 cars' right in the middle of the intersection. As you walk into the bar the bottom part of the bar is kind of broken up into 3 parts. To the left is the stage, D.J. booth and the dance floor/audience area during a show. The middle part is just the bar area with 2 bars and the right side has sitting and a pool table. There are 2 ways to get to the upstairs part of the bar. The first way is the stairs by the front door and the second way is through the smoke area which is enclosed to protect us from the weather. It is not very big but it is nice. This area has a bar downstairs and steps leading upstairs. This is a smoking area and since the world has it in for smokers this is a great place because it is inside. Upstairs is where I like to go it has 2 bars on the one side and a dance floor and the D.J. booth on the other side.

Michael said I would not like this bar at all because he knew I would be uncomfortable. Funny, as it turns out Chris's is my favorite bar today, but at the time he was right it was a bit uncomfortable. In the beginning alcohol helped me through the night. This was a gay bar for men. Men are much different in behaviors they express in the club then women do. They are very physical towards each other and they do not understand personal space. Well, they didn't have the same definition of personal space as I do; a clear bubble at least an arm's length in all directions is mine. As they walked by you they put their hands anywhere. Turns out when a gay man grabs your nipples they are just saying hello. Something else that I learned very quickly that was way out of my comfort zone was gay people are the huggy type of people. I am not. I am used to it now but at first I so was not.

One night at Chris's I met a very wonderful man there named Allen. He was really fun to talk to and he was really cute. He used to be a stripper and trust me when I say he has kept up on the body. He has flawless coco colored skin and tight curls. He is a bit short but that just makes his appeal even that much better. He has a wonderful loving personality. He is so full of energy and let me tell you he can dance. Over the years he has earned a very special place in my heart. Anyway, I would sit behind Allen's table where he was selling his underwear. Allen ran an underwear business where he sold the more tastefully done risqué underwear. He could take one look at you and tell you what size you were and what type of underwear you would look good in.

Sitting behind his table helped me stay inside my safe bubble. As the night went on I ventured out and sat against the wall beside the table. Wayne was there again. Wayne was a blonde haired, nice looking, very muscular, and younger than my husband by about 5 years. Wayne wanted my husband. The one Michael wanted to hook up with and the one he was forced to kiss. Michael came up to me towards the end of the night and told me he wanted to dance with Wayne. I said ok even though I wanted to dance with my husband.

I didn't like to watch them dance together because it made me very uncomfortable. It is very hard watching someone you love show attention towards someone else knowing he wanted to sleep with him. They were dancing very sexually. At this point in our marriage things were ok. I was beginning to get a handle on how I really fit into this whole other world.

Michael and I had many talks and in the end it was always my feelings he was concerned about. I knew Wayne was just a toy but that still didn't help the way I felt. My heart just hurt. In my eyes Michael never danced like that with me or looked at me that way. Remember when I talked about ripples, writing this now brings back those feelings even though it happened years ago and I know the outcome already. Ripples never really go away.

He would give me looks from the dance floor to let me know he loved me which helped. The smiles I was giving him though were insecure ones because of all the things running through my head. I was my worst enemy. I knew my husband loved me and we needed to show the people at the bar that I was ok and that he could be himself while I was there. I understood work was work and had no problem with that. Dancing with Wayne was not, in my eyes, work. Dancing with Wayne was fun. I know dancing with Wayne showed people that I was ok with everything so I guess it was work. The fact was I just needed my heart to catch up with logic. So I smiled because I loved him and moved on.

One night at Chris's when I was a bit more comfortable about being there I met an older man while I was walking around upstairs. He asked me to sit and chat with him. He told me that he had heard a rumor that Michael and I were married and asked if it was true. I confirmed the rumor and he smiled. He said, "Good for you," with a smirk on his face and ordered us a shot. He began telling me about his life.

He bought us another shot and sat there for a second before he continues with this very sad story. He too had been married once a long time ago. When his wife found out she couldn't handle the news. He told me he felt betrayed and hurt so bad he retreated into himself. She left and took their kids with her. He went on to say that she was the only one he would ever love. Being left to deal with his feelings towards her and then his need for men he was forced to only act on his gay side. He knew that there was no way that he could ever love another woman and he would never find a woman who would understand the need he had for men.

He also knew he couldn't give up men. For him to become gay was his only option. At the time he was gay because people in the world were not very accepting. He told me if she had only understood and let him just step out once in a while he would not have to go through all this suffering. He told me that because of this he became very bitter for a long time and that is why he was alone. He would never have someone who would be there to grow old with. Now his wife and kids interact with him but he had already missed most of their lives but he did not want to miss out on his grandkids.

He said I brought hope for the world because I was willing to allow my husband to step out of our marriage to fix what he needed to fix. I was accepting of him even though he knew he was doing wrong because when you are in a marriage you are not supposed to cheat on your wife. He also explained why I and Michael would never fully fit in. He told me Michael wasn't fully gay because he had a wife and kids to go home to. This meant Michael could step out into the gay world to get his fix and then go home to his straight life where his wife and kids were waiting for him. He would never understand or deal with what it means to be gay because he wasn't part of it. Michael could be gay in the gay world but in the "real" world he didn't have to deal with anything. He would never understand because he would never experience the full weight of what it meant to be gay in a straight world.

The gentleman went on to tell me that I pointed out what they would never be...married. They would never have someone who they could take care of and who would take care of them. They would never have a wife who would have their kids and one day have grandkids with. I would always be the slap in the face of things they could never have but at the same time I was telling everyone by my being there ... there is hope for everyone.

When he was done we shared another shot together and he left after giving me a hug. I felt odd after that conversation and wondered if that is how they really saw me and Michael. Over the years I have been told that more than once on all ends of the story so I guess it is true in a way. I never set out to hurt anyone and I had to hope that they understood that.

What he and others have said make some of the peoples actions a bit more understandable, especially the older guys. I noticed this because of the way I got treated at first and still do from some. I will get talked over when we go out of town by most club owners or patrons that I run into. They will talk to Michael but ignore me or pacify me with a smile. I never really understood how hard the gay population had it and in some cases still do. The senseless beating for just being gay is unconscionably. The persecution they have to endure sometimes on a daily basis. The ridicule from people can be relentless. I never really heard about any of it. I do not watch the news very much so I figured people had just gotten over it. I guess they haven't.

Now I don't fully understand the want or need for the same sex because I don't have that glitch. The stories I have heard about the crap gay people have had to put up with though are totally uncalled for. The camps people send their kids to which are run by so called "Christians" in the hope they will come out straight. To bully someone just because they are different is wrong and it pisses me off. The parents of gay children who don't just embrace their children and love them no matter who they are should not be a parent. All parents don't like what their kids do and sometimes we don't even like them but we should always love them no matter what. As parents we should stop our children from making other children feel bad about themselves no matter what the reasons are. Now not everyone treated me badly or just blew me off but a lot did and still do.

This brings in one of my friend Blake. He is a very nice looking man with dark hair and eyes and very well built. He has a very nice smile that light up his eyes when he gets excited. At first he was just a bar tender who was not mean to me but really never talked to me. Over time, though, he and I have had many conversations about a great many things. He is extremely intelligent. Others think he is stuck on himself but once you get to know him and not as just a piece of meat he is a great guy. He is just a guy who knows himself and knows what he wants. He danced before but because people saw him and treated him like a stupid piece of meat he quit. I have asked him questions over the years because he never looks down on me for asking and he is always been honest with me. I feel honored to call him a friend. He has a very cute and adorable boyfriend. He looks like the boy next door but has a heart of gold but I am getting ahead of myself because at this time in the story I had not met him yet. All I will say is that I hope all of Blakes' dreams work out for him. He is one of a few that have treated me with kindness and actually took the time to get to know me and for that I will always love him.

There are other people who have taken the time to get to know me and I am happy to call them my friends now, like Frank. He has a long gray ponytail and beard. He has a heart of gold and over the years I have got to know him better and the more I learn the more I like him. Funny though for the longest time I didn't know he didn't wear pants. The bar owner has stopped that though now but one night out of the blue I realized he wasn't wearing any pants. Blake, Michael and Frank just laughed because I had been going there for 3 years by this time and had never noticed. The two people that run the bar is Mike and Liz. I was nervous about Liz since up till this point I have not had good luck with lesbians but Liz is nice. She is quiet and I don't know much about her but I like her. Mike is a very tall man which is funny the man he is with is called little Mike. He is so nice and we have shared recipes over the years. The other two bar tenders upstairs really never talked to me but I could tell that they were nice. The last person I am going to mention is a very dear friend of mine… Gary. He stole my heart the moment I met him. He is a powerhouse of personality in a tiny body and I love it. Ok, sorry way off track…I just love talking about people who make me happy. So, let's see where I was oh yea… the fashion show.

The next time we went out it was to Tom's for a fashion show. We had bought me a new pink shirt which I thought I looked very good in. Michael had asked if I could take pictures of the fashion show for him. I figured I was just sitting there I could do that. I knew Michael would be backstage a lot which would give me something to do instead of just sitting there. I was right Michael and the other models spent most of the night backstage. This was the first time I learned about gay time. The show was supposed to start at 8 and at 9 I asked Allen what was going on and he laughed and told me nothing was we are just running on gay time. The show didn't start till 11. After that I was fully aware of gay time. So just FYI … If you want to meet someone at 8 tell them 7 so they will be there at 8:30.

The show finally started and I had a perfect seat. I was sitting center stage right up front. I had the perfect spot to take pictures. Little did I know this was the danger zone! The show started with the main drag queen coming out to the stage and beginning the show with her monologue. His make-up was fiery red bouffant hair and 50's style horned rim glasses with make-up way over the top like Mimi from the Drew Cary show. As soon as he started he spotted me and it was on. He began to coax me up on stage. I didn't want to go but I quickly learned they don't take no for an answers just so you know. I learned three things that night. 1. You can't see anything when you're on stage because of all the lights blinding you. 2. Never wear a bright colored shirt and sit close to the stage. 3. Men even gay men love boobs, the bigger the better. I found that to be odd but it is the truth.

Not sure why this is other than for maybe shock value. That night I was still very uncomfortable about it all but I was a good sport. Mr. Glass told Michael that I got pulled up on stage and that it was funny and I played along like a champ before I ever got the chance to tell him. Which brings up another point…gossip runs amuck. Don't do anything you don't want the rest of the gay community to know. With it being a small community everyone knows everyone else which means things travel fast in the gay world.

Now remember that drag queen that did the Lady GaGa song with Michael and Wayne let me tell you more about her so you can form your opinion about her. While the boys were backstage she was trying to hook up with my husband and Wayne. She was rubbing all over them. She was trying to get a cheap feel rubbing on their legs and all over their chest. Now I know what my husband finds attractive and that is not it. Although that didn't stop her from telling everyone that she did them both in the back. Scott actually had to call her out on all of her shit in front of everyone to make her stop telling people that story. I can't blame her/him I am sure he never gets anyone that looks as good as they do. My problem is don't lie. Now you tell me what type of drag queen she is…if you could see her there would be no question.

Scott only got the guys gogo gigs. They all saw Michael as the leader and would contact him about other stuff. He would then tell Scott but Scott never really planned for the guys to do anything major. Scott was happy with just having them dance at clubs and him going. Michael wanted them to be more and even talked to Scott about it.

CHAPTER 8

My next outing was Pride. The reason why Pride was created was so that all gay people, that would include lesbians…I'll explain later why I said that, to come together in celebration. PRIDE was started to unify they gay community. PRIDE was a way for the gay community and their supporters to come together in celebration without being looked down upon. Most events are for the straight community where gay people are welcome as long as they behave in a manner in which everyone around finds acceptable… straight acting. They are a group of people, human beings, which have been through a lot. In the past if you were gay you could be killed and in some places today it is still that way. There are still random beatings going on in today's world. Pride is a place where they can celebrate who they are and who they love with others in the community and supporters.

PRIDE from everything I know, personally, in pictures, and have heard from others in the community this is not what PRIDE is now. Yes it is a celebration of being gay but it is more for the young ones to let loose and exclaim to the world whether any one likes it or not they are gay. It is a way for the bars to make money. A drunken sex driven event is what it has become. Most of the people I know don't even participate in PRIDE for these reasons. It is like Irish Fest because it has turned into a 3 day drunk.

I have talked and listened to a lot of people about PRIDE and one thing that sticks out is how they are trying to make PRIDE kid friendly. I am not sure why they are trying to do this because most of them do not have kids. I would never take my kids to a party I am not sure why others want to. To me PRIDE is a time where the gay community can be out in public and act any way the want to at any time with no worries…so why would you want kids there. To me they are trying to make it kid friendly for all the straight people who come. Anyway getting off my soap box and I will get on with the story.

J.R. a DJ Michael met at Chris's asked him and the boys to dance for PRIDE. This was a big deal for Michael and the boys. For me though, I was not that excited. For Michael and the boys I was happy. I was not excited at all because this was my husband and father of my children. I was nervous and scared someone would find out. Dancing at a gay bar where only gay people went, or so I thought, was one thing. PRIDE was going to be at a straight venue actually an extremely straight venue.

My fear was that a parent at my little girl's school would be there and recognize Michael. That would cause her problems. Some of you reading this are thinking … no it would not… it would and I'll explain. I know that people pass judgment on things they do not understand. I experienced that because when I went out trust me I had ideas in my head on how things were supposed to be and they were not that way. I have talked to other straight people and they have told me that they do not want gay people around their kids because their moral compass is off and they are sexual deviant's especially gay men. I have heard these things for myself so I know that if people found out about my husband my daughter will suffer because of the kids' parents.

Yes, sex is a big part of the gay man mentality but that doesn't make them pedophiles. I don't want my daughter to deal with the crap I know she would. I did not want the news of her dad dancing at PRIDE for a bunch of men to get around my daughters school and have her friends parents not let their kids come to her birthday parties because of her dad. Not to mention the teasing she would endure from the close minded bigots and bible thumpers infecting their children's minds.

Michael and I had a lot of talks about this and finally we agreed he would do it. He explained to me and it is true that in the bigger cities there are straight men dancing in gay bars for money. I was going to be there so if anything was said we could tell them that it was for the money. The term gay for pay comes from this type of behavior and porn. When you see a snapshot of something you can make up any story in your head which may not even come close to the real story.

I had fun that night watching him dance on stage. I was so proud of him. It takes a lot of guts to get up and dance for thousands of people. I took pictures of the act; I had started doing that when I went out with Michael. J.R.'s music was great it had everyone dancing. The boy's looked great. This was Michael's first time on stage. You would have never known it because he looked like a pro. It wasn't liquid courage either. I should know because we only had one drink that night. It was a lame weak drink that took us 45 minutes to get because walking from the stage area to the bar and back took us that long. The place was packed.

We were all standing back stage waiting to go on. Michael and I were going to have a date night after the show. I was so looking forward to it. It had been a long time and with everything we had been thru I was excited to spend some time just with him.

They were all doing push-ups and getting ready. Rick, one of the dancers stole my heart. Have you ever been friends with anyone who was just so open and honest about themselves? That is Rick. He told me that he was never really teased at school for being gay and he was the popular kid. He loved life and trying to improve himself all the time. Money was a major factor in everything he did. He was a free spirit and I loved that about him. He was completely comfortable with himself and if you were not comfortable with him then that was your problem. Oddly enough he didn't like hair because he shaved all of his off even his eyebrows. He looked good without them actually. His coco skin was flawless. He is beautiful in every way. He is very slender but tone and very flexible the things I have seen him do make me wonder if he has any bones in his body.

So the boys went out on stage and I went around to the front area of the stage to get ready to take pictures. A woman I had run into before walked up to me and asked about some badge I did not have. She told me I was going to have to leave if I didn't have one. I told her I was there taking pictures of the boys. She told me she didn't care and that I still needed to get on the other side of the gate. Just then the gentleman who was president of pride came over to see what was going on. When he saw me he grabbed me and gave me a hug and asked how I was as he grabbed my boob. I told him fine. The woman began telling him that the straight girl didn't have a pass. He cut her off and handed me his and said now she does move on. He turned back to me and told me that my husband looked hot in the underwear he was wearing and how he would like to see them crumpled up on his floor. She turned and walked away.

I should mention that this was the same woman who only a few weeks ago gave me and a deaf guy a hard time at the fashion show. She was standing behind him and was telling him that she wanted to move the tables. When he didn't jump up and move she became very rude and just started to move the table which startled him. I stood up and told her he was deaf and that she did not need to be so rude. She looked at me and told me to mind my own business. Someone walked over and said something to her about me being Michael's wife and she said fu##ing straight people. I was shocked because I was there supporting a gay event that was helping to raise money for PRIDE and AID's. This was actually my first time really ever dealing with a lesbian. You could say I was not happy and figured if they were all like this I wouldn't have much to do with them. Oddly I have only met a select few lesbians that I even like.

Now let's get back to the night of PRIDE and the boys on stage. The boys put on a great show for the crowd. Rick, now remember I told you he was extremely flexible now you will know why. On stage he did this sexually erotic backbend where he was sandwiched between Wayne and Michael. He was straddling Wayne and went into a backbend where he looked like he was going down on Michael. This made the crowd go crazy. Rick had a way of working the crowd. It was amazing to watch. Over the years Michael and Rick worked well together but I'm getting a head of myself.

People got pulled up on stage to dance with the boys. Everyone was having a great time. They were having such a good time that they almost collapsed the platform the boys were dancing on. Not to mention they almost knocked the boys off. Everyone wanted a piece of the boys. They all did a great job I was so proud of my husband and the job they did.

The DJ we were working for, J.R., was a very nice man and hired us for many other things over the next few years. He was a very interesting man with a variety of interests. It was very sad when he died a few years later. Over the years I had opportunities to talk with him on a personal level and he had a heart of gold. You will be missed.

After that show we were supposed to have a date night and stay where they performed but Wayne needed us to walk him back. I didn't understand why he couldn't ride with Rick or walk 3 blocks by himself but whatever.

There were a few times during the beginning that I felt my husband was very insensitive to me and this would be one of the times. I will explain in a bit more detail and you will understand.

As we were leaving J.R. called to me and motioned for me to come back. I yelled at Michael to wait and walked back to J.R. He wanted to thank us and tell us we did a great job. He gave me a hug and told me it was wonderful to meet me. When I turned around my husband was nowhere to be seen. When I did find him he was walking out the gate with Wayne. Wayne noticed I was not there and stopped Michael. After they finally stopped and waited on me I was able to catch up. Walking back he walked up with Wayne. They walked ahead of me instead of with me. This made me feel like a third wheel. They hardly talked to me I was just the tag along.

The club we were walking back to was the same one we had left not more than 3 hours ago. Wayne couldn't find his way back even though we walked the same way we walked to PRIDE. When I heard this well, you can imagine what I thought. You're right…dumbass…that was what I was thinking.

Then during our date Michael kept watching him dance. I wanted to go downstairs; actually I wanted to go anywhere where Wayne wasn't. There was a group performing downstairs so we went down there to watch and they were good. The woman singing was also maneuvering a hula hoop all around her body at the same time she was singing. She even laid down on the floor and stood back up and the hula hoop never stopped. She was amazing. The rest of the group did small aerobatics in long sheets of material. They put on a good show.

Michael and I look at the night differently because he said that it didn't mean anything and to me it showed me that he wasn't taking my feelings into consideration. After all we had been through and everything I was dealing with on a personal level I wanted more. So far I expected him to be a bit more attentive and look at how I felt not just dismissing it because it didn't mean anything to him. It wasn't just his relationship it was mine too.

Let me explain a bit more. I know that I am an attractive woman and I am a hell of a person but with all the crap I had been through my self-esteem had dropped slightly. I had never been a jealous person but because I had just lost 3 babies and dealing with depression I wasn't the old me anymore. I had a life changing event with the twins for the better but for what he was doing we were not in sync anymore. I enjoyed the change in my life spiritually but mentally and physically there had been a toll taken. I had gained weight so I wasn't the skinny thing I had always been. During my vulnerable times my husband had lied to me and told me that he wasn't sure he wanted to stick around. If you have never been put in that situation then you cannot really understand the amount of confusion and how that affects your mental thinking.

Something else I should add in here is that he was wrong. He knew what he was doing was wrong and admitted it. I mean the cheating and lying in our marriage. So because of these things he understood where I was coming from. Unfortunately, it just did not come across that way in our conversations or in his actions. It was hard for me to get him to understand that all I wanted was some attention. The kind of attention I had been missing since all this had started. I knew he knew these things but because he is sometimes a bit bullheaded he didn't say it or think about it before he did something.

So for a while, I was not myself mentally and all this was very hard. I was trying to pull myself out of a hole I didn't know how to get out of. When you see your husband paying attention to someone else in a way that he doesn't pay attention to you it makes your mind think all sorts of things. I always knew deep down that we would be ok but all the stuff going on makes you doubt things that you know.

I had decided that enough was enough and I began to fight back for me. I started going to the gym and boxing and kickboxing. If you want a way to lose weight and help with your frustration level take boxing and kickboxing it does wonders. I loved how it took away my frustrations and after class I was a new person. I was beginning to see the old me once again. Michael was the instructor so it was something he and I could do together outside of the world he was in. This was something that was just ours with nobody else there. Unfortunately, it didn't stay that way. Michael came to me one day and told me that Wayne wanted to come and take class with us.

So here is this muscle guy who my husband finds sexually attractive taking class with his over-weight, fighting depression wife. Yup you're right I was not happy. I tried to get him to understand that but he didn't. This just pissed me off. I will admit that the workout that day was great because it was

Michael that day I was beating the shit out of. On a side note I did better at the class then Wayne did. Raise your hands up and say Woop Woop.

At this time in my life I was tired of sharing my husband with what I felt was the gay community. All the time spent on the computer talking to all his gay friends, booking massage clients and watching porn clips, searching all the sites and looking at hot men was time not spent with me or the family. This was a life I was not part of and it was only shared with me to a point. I would say things to him and he would get off the computer for a bit but wanted right back on. I was the one with the problem according to Michael not him. I have always said of course you don't have a problem it is not being done to you but for the most part I felt it fell on deaf ears.

So now here is this guy who my husband wants to hook up with taking class with me. He was invading my world. I had to share all aspects of my husband with the gay community and now it was creeping in on my straight world. I was not happy and that is putting it mildly.

So after class we went to get something to eat like we always did but this time Michael invited Wayne. After sitting there talking for about an hour I saw Wayne put his hand on my husband's thigh. Michael moved it off but I had already seen it. I was done, not only was our daughter there but it was totally inappropriate. Public displays of affection from anyone Michael or I feel are not appropriate. Your private life should remain that … PRIVATE. A quick kiss maybe or holding hands for a few minutes is fine but there is a time and a place for anything else.

When I saw his hand I felt that it was disrespectful to me and to our daughter. We were sitting right there. I stood up and said, "We need to leave and we are going to the car," to which I took our daughters hand and walked out. The longer my husband stayed in there talking the madder I got. My husband came out about 10 to 15 minutes later. I was so mad by then but couldn't say anything because our daughter was in the car but when we got home and she was in bed I told him that I didn't want him to have anything to do with Wayne and he was off limits as far as hooking up.

The next run in with Wayne was when my oldest called us from jail and I was very upset but my husband decided to go and talk to Wayne. I do not excuse the selfish behavior but I do understand it a bit better now. Michael was a kid in a candy store. At first everything was hands off but now he could touch, Michael and Wayne never did anything except a bit of groping on each other but Wayne was out with no strings except for a boyfriend if that is what you want to call it. Michael had just started to experience this. Here was this muscular guy who was interested in Michael and Michael was interested in him. So he was letting his little head control the head on his shoulders.

There came many talks after that about how I saw things going and how we could work things out together. One of the rules I came up with was if I have more balls then they do then they are a no go. See I was going to be the only woman in Michaels' life and when I was more masculine then the man was there was a problem. Not to mention the disrespect I felt being in a public place with my husband and child with someone putting their hand where their hand should never be … on my husband's thigh in front of my child. On a side note a few months later my husband thought about him the same way and oddly enough most everyone does.

Ok, let me stop here just for a moment. Wayne was only a small part of what I went through that summer so now I will explain the rest of it to you. I am going to go through it in the order of how it happened but understand it took place during 4 or 5 months and Pride and Wayne fell within that timeline. Now remember at the beginning of this summer our marriage was a bit rocky and we had lost our home and had to move in with a friend of ours. The first thing that I found out was that Michael had cheated on me.

You know when your gut tells you something is just not right…well you should listen to yourself. You know better than anyone what is going on in your life and around you. One problem Michael and I had was him taking care of himself in the shower leaving me high and dry. Every time I got a feeling I was right. Once again I had a feeling that he was keeping something from me. While he was in the shower I found an email from one of his massage clients that talked about how much he enjoyed sex with Michael and how he couldn't wait till the next time they were together.

I believed him when he told me that the most that ever happened with his clients is that he had jacked some of them off sometimes and let them play with him while he gave them a massage. I didn't care about any of that. After our talk when he said he would let me wrap my head around the idea of him stepping out again I believed him. Even after all the lies he had told me I believed him. Yes, I know this makes me look like a stupid bitch and if you know anything about me I do not like when people think I am stupid because trust me I am not. Like I said before if our marriage was going to work I had to be the one to start down the trusting road so that we could get back to where we needed to be.

Now I find out that once again he did what he wanted to do and didn't care how it would affect me. I cried the whole time he was in the shower. Mainly because I wanted to kill him for taking advantage of me and the lack of respect he showed me and our relationship. If I cannot kill you I cry. I couldn't keep doing this. I couldn't let him do whatever he wanted without taking my feelings and our relationship into consideration

When he got out I asked him who this guy was and he said a client. I also asked if all he did with him was give him a message, Michael knows me well enough to know I normally don't ask direct questions like that unless I already know the answer; so he didn't lie. He told me it was only one time and that it just happened it was nothing planned. He told me he was sorry and that he wouldn't do a massage for him again. Michael also knows my weak spot. If he can get within my bubble of comfort and just talk to me all I want to do is hug him not stab him. I had been going along with no problems but every time something comes up it brings it all back again and we are at square one again. You would think Michael would learn that but this type of relationship doesn't come with a manual and I have never met anyone else with our type of relationship so we were winging it. Sometimes things work out sometimes they don't.

I know what you're thinking. Well I would never forgive him. You have to look at the bigger picture. We have so much history together and we think so much alike that it is hard to just give up on your soul mate. I knew this will not go on forever because he will get old and in the gay world unless you look a certain way you are not wanted any more. I also knew that this subject is a hard one to talk about especially trying to tell the woman you love that you need something she cannot give you. It is hard to watch your husband ache for something you cannot help him with. There is a lot of emotions that go into this marriage and neither one of us are blind to that. That is not to say we don't get tunnel vision sometimes on things but we really are there for each other and do not want the other to hurt.

I am not some weak minded stupid woman like you see on Jerry Springer. This subject and what we have chosen to do cannot be looked at in black and white. Yes, I wanted to believe him. I wanted him to be comfortable enough to be able to tell me everything. When you're not comfortable with yourself then how can you be comfortable with anyone? This subject is hard and it is not easy to just blurt things out.

Yes, I wanted all this crap to be over. I know that he had a glitch and it wasn't his fault I was taking too long. It is not something I just thought of everyday with the intentions of walking up to him and saying, "Yes honey you may step out". Yes, he should have waited but I should have been more understanding because I knew it was a problem for him and after all the times he had been supportive to me especially during the loss of the twins I wasn't helping. When he lied to me and began sneaking around this didn't help my situation at all. It was these behaviors I was having a hard time with. I read through other email and there were not any email saying anything I was uncomfortable with this guy was just a toy a means to an end.

Another point is what we call cheating. Sex can be just that, sex. Cheating is being with another person where there is a chance to replace the one your with or an emotional connection with another person behind someone's back or hiding the fact that it is going on. Any of those things means you're cheating on the one you're with. Using someone of the same sex for sex means they are just a toy. Black and white…yes they are cheating but Michael and I don't see what he does as cheating it is just like using a toy when I'm not around only this toy actually moves.

I understood the toy philosophy because I had done that more times than I care to admit. A toy is a toy. So when it comes down to it as long as that is all they are used for neither Michael nor I see it as cheating. In our relationship because Michael does not want anything from them but sex, a way to get off or a release that I cannot give him since I do not have that part it is just…sex and not considered cheating. It works for us so what everyone else thinks we really do not care.

I know my husband would not be ok with them being anything else but a toy. He is not the boyfriend kind of guy. He could only stand dealing with soft qualities like crying, cuddling, sometimes being needy behavior from a women. He couldn't stand this from another man. So because of how we feel this works for us.

The next thing I went through was something that blew me away. In all our years so far there was only a minute thought of being free for me because we were not in a good place. The thought left as soon as it came into my head so what was about to happen broke my heart. I began to notice that there was something wrong with my husband. He looked and acted distant. Sex was not happening at all. We were living with my friend still so I understood that part but he wasn't even acting like a husband should act.

One night I told him I needed to know what was going on with him. He began to explain to me that he wasn't sure he wanted to be with me and the kids anymore because of his bi side and the way he was feeling and how it was affecting me. He couldn't devote 100% to me because of the part of him that ate away at him about the other men. He couldn't fix that part of him and didn't really want to try. He wanted to experience more of it and didn't want to hurt me. He knew he was in the wrong and didn't want to ask his wife for any more than I had already given. He didn't want to look at the hurt and disappointment on my face.

He told me he didn't want a relationship with another man. That I was the only person he would ever want to have a relationship with. He felt horrible putting me through anymore stuff or causing me problems because of his glitch. He loved me more than anything and he didn't want to leave or loose me because of his problem. Michael told me that he was just thinking about it and had not made a decision.

He had been talking to a friend of his about it. His friend had told him to weigh all his options. What would leaving me mean…was it worth losing everything for a side that would end with him being alone. Turns out he told him that it was Michael's decision and he would have to live with whatever decision he made. To do what made him happy…if it was staying married then stay married and figure out how to live with the need he had or leave me and the kids and deal with whatever happens with that.

Turns out that was the best advice for him. He became a good friend to both of us and I am really glad Michael had him to talk to because he took his feelings out of it and just gave him good advice. I know that was hard for him to do because he liked my husband. Most people would have told him to leave because of their own selfish needs but this wonderful man gave him honest advice which led to him staying with me.

We talked for a long time that night. I told him that if he did leave than what he was saying wasn't true. If I was willing to stay with him after all the bullshit I had already been through then I must love him more. I was willing to try and figure something out and if he was going to throw that all away then what he didn't really love me the way he said he did. I didn't mean that much to him. I told him that all we needed to do was just figure out a way to make it work.

He couldn't have free reign because he was married. The most important thing was as long as we did love each other than we could work through anything. We needed to talk about everything, putting each other first, no more lies about anything and no more cheating at all. If we did all these things we could make it through anything together because we had already been through so much.

We both cried, me more, it was a very emotional conversation between us. During the conversation I could see how much it hurt him to say these things especially because of everything we had been through, which he mentioned several times. So to tell me anything it bothered him. I love my husband with all my heart and I was not willing to give up my best friend, lover, and father of my kids because he had an issue and a glitch that could be fixed with a toy once a month. The conversation ended with uneasy feelings.

Not knowing what lies ahead because you are not in control of your own life makes you feel like you are walking on a high wire without a net. The next month was hard for me. When you feel disconnected from someone it leaves you unsure of what to do. I was not use to that. For the first time in our marriage I took steps just in case it didn't end well for me and the kids. I called my sister to see if we could stay with her. I knew I couldn't stay anywhere around him because if it didn't work out it would just be too hard for me to see him. Especially knowing everything we had been through and how much I loved him and our children loved him and for him to choose his bi side over us really upset me. There would be no way that I could look at him because to me that would mean that he loved sex with men more than me and the kids. I was willing to deal with him having a toy and had forgiven him for cheating and he chose to leave then he was not even close to loving me as much as I love him.

In a very tender moment he came to me and told me to stop worrying. He told me that he was not going anywhere he loved me and loved being married to me. He wanted things to work between us but he wasn't sure how it was going to work out. If anyone was going to end the marriage it was going to be me not him because he was in it till the end. I still worried a little but not as much because the look on his face was one of peace. It was nice to know he had come to a decision that he was happy with the decision he had made for his life.

We both knew that our life together was something that was worth fighting for. We both knew that a marriage is not just a piece of paper. We both take our vows the way they are supposed to be taken. You cannot just give up on the ones you love. To be together you have to love all of them even the flaws. As an individual we have to look at the whole picture and be secure in our own mind what is most important. Other than this small part of his personality he was what I wanted.

A few weeks after that Michael came to me and asked if he could meet a buddy. I said yes. I was nervous because I worried about what would happen but after our talk I wanted to be supportive. I kissed him good-bye and watched him drive away. A friend of my daughters had come down to visit and he and I stood outside talking. Before I knew it my husband was pulling back in the drive. I was shocked that it had already been 2 hours. I kissed him and life went on. This is how buddies should be…well there are a few we will talk about later…but 1 day out of a year was really no big deal. I and we would be fine. I say one day out of the year because when you figure 2 hours a month times 12 you get 24 hours. Most women would like to get rid of their husbands for more than that so it was all good.

We were going to open a gym. We had everything, trainers, equipment, a building, and programs for the computer and a backer who would help us pull it all together. We were excited. We got a small place so that our bills would not be high and it was just big enough for the 3 of us because our oldest had already moved out. The economy didn't feel the same so when it bottomed out so did the backer and we were left with nothing.

It was a hard time for money but we would be fine. I know money issues are hard on a marriage and ours is no different. Michael picked up more clients that carried us through. One night I was, we don't remember why I got on the computer for him but anyway, I was on his email. I began to read some of them and found several emails from clients that talked about the sex they had with my husband. Thank goodness our youngest was asleep because I was devastated. All I could think about was what a fool I had been by believing him all this time. I'm not sure what I was feeling or thinking really because I was empty. There were so many thoughts running through my mind that it was hard to keep a thought in my head. I knew that when he got home we needed to talk. I knew that he now was lying to me again but how far did it go…. were some of these people just buddies and he was telling me they were clients because I never checked the money when he got home. How far back was it…since the beginning…it would explain why sex for us dropped off.

When he got home I just asked him and he confirmed what I already knew. With tears in his eyes he told me that in the beginning it was just a massage but he wasn't getting any repeat business and with him being the only one working he had to do something to take care of us and pay the bills. He told me he would do it again whether I liked it or not because he needed to take care of his family. I understood that he did what he had to.

I think I should take some time to really explain clients to you. The best way to explain them is to explain some of the situations. Some might be what you think but most are just lonely people. They are unattractive or busy people who cannot get or have time to find anyone to hook up with. Not to mention all the BS you have to go through just to have sex. I will say that one post on a social media account my husband has summed it all up. This guy was mad at his date because his date asked him if he was hungry and wanted to get something to eat and when he said no the guy drove thru a fast food place and grabbed something for himself. This guy went on and on about how rude it was that this guy ate something and if he had said yes he was hungry then this guy would have taken him to a fast food place. Sounds like what most guys go through with girls. I saw it as this guy was hungry the date was not so he quickly got something to eat so they could start the date. Anyway some clients do not have time for all that crap all they want is human companionship. At first doing this made Michael feel cheap but then something happened that changed his mind.

Michael placed an ad on Craigs List and an older man answered the ad. When Michael showed up he texted the man the man texted back that he was sorry but his sister had shown up and asked if Michael could wait. Michael waited about 15 minutes for her to leave. When she did Michael went in and introduced himself in a way to help put the guys mind at ease. The man's hair was fading into gray and he was in his 40's.

The pleasantries continued as they walked to the bedroom. Michael asked the guy to undress and lie on his belly so he could begin the massage and asked if he wanted Michael to undress. The client told Michael that he had cancer before he got undressed because he had a colostomy bag. The client apologized saying he knew it was gross. Michael assured him it was fine. The client went on to say that his boyfriend had left him after he found out he had cancer. His sister wanted him to move in with her so she could take care of him. He wasn't sure if he wanted to give up his independence just yet. He knew that the time was coming because he was very ill. His condition and the things he couldn't do for himself made him understand that he wouldn't be able to stay by himself much longer. He just didn't want his situation to take away his last little bit of freedom just yet.

Michael knew why he was there and so did the client. This was going to be the last human touch on an intimate level this man was going to have. After it was all said and done and Michael was leaving he felt very heavy hearted and slightly honored that he was what the man choose to be with in the end. Michael did a lot of thinking on the way home and began to see his client in a different light.

Like the gay man who was scared to have sex. He would invite Michael over and all they would do is slide around each other in baby oil. He knew anyone else would want it to go further. He even bought Michael underwear so he would not ruin his. They would talk about a lot of things. The man was a school teacher and taught 4th grade and just needed human contact. Now imagine going out and picking up someone else and telling them you didn't want sex you just wanted to rub on each other...how long do you think that date would stay around. Michael didn't judge him and made him feel comfortable.

The man that ran a million dollar business hired Michael for the same reason. This client didn't have time to meet anyone and if he did they always wanted him for his money. Michael had no real part in his life. Michael served his purposes and that is it. This client had been married before and still had the urge to take care of someone but just couldn't do that to another man. Men are supposed to be the ones to take care of the other half but not another man.

Many of his clients are like this. People with problems, hang-up's, phobias, or issues that only someone like Michael could solve. We all pass judgment on people because of their choices. Why, if it is not hurting you then why pass judgment on them for something they like. Michael took on clients for the money to help his family survive but it turns out that he found an odd satisfaction in helping others.

You may look down on him for this but I don't. I have met some of these client and they are wonderful people. Everyone can understand the feeling of being lonely and needing someone. I understand wanting to do anything for your family. I have so much respect for my husband for doing everything he could to make sure we had a roof over our head and food in our stomach. In today's world where you are not paid what your worth it was nice to know that my husband took care of us.

Electric won't wait 2 maybe 3 weeks to collect on their bill while you find a job and then get paid from that job. Your kids can't go that long without food. We are not talking money to go out on or dine in a restaurant we are talking about school clothes, food, rent and utilities. You are probably the one who would arrest the mother for stealing bread and lunch meat to feed her kids. Stealing is wrong but shit happens and sometimes you cannot control the world around you and you become down on your luck. So as everyone knows you do what you have to so you survive. I am not talking about the thugs who are to lazy to get a job and they rob people or sell drugs I am talking about the people who are really trying to get ahead they just keep falling short.

I felt horrible that he was doing that to take care of us. I told him I was sorry that he felt he had to do. He had some bad feelings about all of this towards me and this lead into a deeper talk which dealt with us losing the last place we lived because he felt like we just saw him as an ATM. Our oldest didn't really help and I didn't have a job so I can understand why he thought that. I told him that I never looked at him like that and I was so sorry he felt like that. I know understood why sex dropped off too. The people he was sleeping with were not his choice and he didn't like all of them so it made him feel dirty. When sex is a job having sex is not on your top 10 list of things you want to do.

We are not delusional about what he does now but the change has been over time for me. No he should not be doing it but we have talked about a lot of things especially clients. His very first client, though, became a very good friend because of the advice he gave Michael without putting selfish reasons into his thinking. For that I will always be grateful. I have actually made Christmas boxes for some of his clients. I know that sounds weird but the ones I did that for were not just clients they had become friends with Michael. They asked about the kids and me and told him to wish us Merry Christmas and Happy Birthday and like I said I have actually met. Michael and his clients know why he is there. They don't talk about it but they both know. The issue for Michael and I in the beginning is we were not talking about things so his feelings were not being understood and I felt very bad about that.

This would be a lack of communication on our part. Communication is the key to any great relationship. To be honest with each other in how you keep misunderstanding to a minimum. There is another behavior that goes hand in hand with a good marriage and that is compromise. Sure you don't want to compromise on who you are but compromising with each other helps in the growth of your relationship is essential. Two people must lean on each other to ensure a healthy relationship. In a marriage both must give up or do things for the other person that they may not like to make sure that their partner in life is happy. Understanding one another is something that every relationship needs. When there are no words spoken you must know them well enough to know what they are thinking. When people tell you things about the other you know if it is true or not because of the understanding the two of you have for one another. I do not hold the clients against my husband in any way, shape or form because I know why he did the things he did.

So anyway.... After Pride Scott began to get them gigs a bit more often and I started going as often as I could. We were invited to Mr. Glass's birthday party. It was so much fun. We bought him the movie Unbreakable because of his nick-name. As a joke someone bought him a princess crown which he wore. Tom the owner and main drag queen of Tom's pulled him up on stage to wish him happy birthday. The bride in the bridal shower did a shot off Mr. Glass's stomach. She was very flirty with him. We all got a kick out of it because she wouldn't even turn his head. We had a blast that night. I always had a great time when I got to go out and hang with Mr. Glass and Brent. It is sad to know they are not together anymore, after many years, but I still see them out sometimes. They are still the best of friends and I hold a secret wish things work out for them again. I see Mr. Glass more than Brent but no matter what they are still two of my favorite people.

That Christmas we went back again to Tom's to enjoy our friends and festivities. We spent the night drinking. JR, Brian, Mr. Glass and Brent were all there. JR was having some issues that he was dealing with. We chatted about it and promised each other we would do lunch but we never got around to it. Mr. Glass was a very happy go lucky type of person but Brent was quieter. Brent would pretty much stay in one spot all night drinking and Mr. Glass would be all over the bar talking to everyone. Mr. Glass knew everyone. I will always have a soft spot for Mr. Glass and Brent for always making me feel welcome.

That next year I threw Michael a surprise birthday party at Chris's. Almost everyone I invited came and it was a great success. Mr. Glass, Brent, Ryan, Chuck, Blane only to name a few. Michael had a great time. He did have one issue because he didn't go out really and everyone wanted time with him and he felt obligated to spend time with everyone instead of just having a good time.

I have become good friends with Chuck. The first time really meeting him was to pick up bail money for my husband. We didn't have tags on the car and we kept getting tickets and didn't pay one of them and he was arrested. I won't get on my soap box about how the cops would sit and wait on us to leave. The first time I actually got to spend time with him I fell in love with his crass wit and sarcasm.

At first I wondered if he liked me for me or because of Michael. He came sometimes to see Michael dance and hang out with me. There were a few times that he never really even talked to Michael and just hung out with me. He went with me to one of Michael's strip shows. I am so glad he did because after he described the bathrooms it saved me the trip. He brought his roommate with him a few times who was a wonderful guy.

Over the years Chuck and I have has some very nice conversations and I feel I can trust him with anything. His roommate Jake is a very sweet, soft hearted man, he is very tall unlike Chuck. Chuck grayed early but he has the nicest hair I love the color. Jake on the other hand has dirty blonde hair. Over the years he has had a few hair styles this latest one I think is the best by far. He is wearing it long and it makes him look dangerous which makes him very attractive.

One night Michael was dancing at Flexx when I got to find out what OMG YOUR MY NEW BFF meant. He was dancing and it was getting late. I was ready for the night to be over. I was sitting minding my own business just waiting to go home. Flexx's wasn't the most fun bar in the world. As the night was getting ready to end this guy wouldn't leave Michael alone. He had been coming up all night talking and groping Michael and Michael though it would be cute to send him over to me to get him off him. I noticed them talking when Michael pointed at me and this guy turned around with this odd look on his face. You know in the movies when panic rushes over someone because they see a very uncomfortable situation about to happen…well this was me. I was hoping that there was someone behind me but I knew there wasn't because my back was against the wall.

This guy ran over to me with kind of a leapy jump to his step with his arms in the air. "Are you really his wife…OMG YOUR MY NEW BFF!", were the first words out of his mouth. Then he grabbed ahold of me and gave me a big hug. All I could do is stand there. He rattled on and on as I gave Michael a death look which he laughed at. Finally the guy said let's have a drink. When the guy left I walked over to where Michael was sitting. Now, because I am me I decided to play a trick on Scott so I walked over to Michael and told him that if he ever did that again I would kill him. Scott had the best look of worry and panic on his face. Michael started laughing and so did I. As I went on with why I said what I did Scott just rolled his eyes and walked away.

This is where I met Blane and Bobby. Two of the nicest and fun loving people you will ever met. They were the DJ's for the event that Michael was dancing for. They were very exciting DJ's with a passion for music and entertaining people.

CHAPTER 9

Blane and Bobby are two of our friends that are perfect for each other. They are both D.J. well actually video D.J.'s. That means that they mix together the videos from the songs and pictures and stuff they really do a great job. They both are very handsome men and a perfect fit. They finish each other's sentences and then just laugh. They work well together and they seem like they are in perfect sync. Unfortunately they got burned by that bar and had to find a new place to play. They were told they could have the weekend to play their music and have a place for everyone to go. Turns out the bar owner wanted to use it as a restaurant instead of being used just on the weekend as a bar. The boys were now looking for a new place to DJ at. They loved being DJ's. They actually now both have their own show on the radio, which I listen to all the time when Michael and I are going out. They played great music so it wasn't long before they found a new place to call home.

The next bar they were told that they could use was a bit off the beaten path. Bottom's had 2 poles one on either of the gogo boxes they had for them to dance on at the far end of the bar. The bar area was split in two parts separated by a half wall. The bigger side of the bar had the bigger bar area that was in the shape of a square and the half wall separated the two half's of the bar. Blane and Bobby had put up video screens and ran new lighting for the bar so their equipment would work. Unfortunately to use their equipment in this other bar they had to rewire everything just to get their equipment to work. Scott brought in Carlos to dance with them. He was a very nice guy but his costumes were out of this world. He was from

Chili so he brought a lot of his culture to his costumes. All his costumes where all home-made and told a story. Sadly he was deported and where he comes from he cannot be gay or he could be killed.

Many things happened at this bar even though it was not open for very long, well at least with the boys doing their thing. I remember one night while Michael was dancing on one of the poles there he ripped up all the calluses to where they were only holding on by the skin at the bottom of his fingers. You could see under them and there were about 1/3 inch ditches in his hands. Michael had to keep it wrapped for weeks.

There was another dancer that started dancing with them around this time named Lance. He was a nice guy and boy did he like to party. Sadly though one night we tried to talk him out of going home with this one guy but we couldn't and that was the last night we saw him for a very long time. About 4 years later we found out that that night did not go very well for him and he entered into rehab and got his life in order.

This is where we first met Pepper Mashay. The bar had a downstairs bar that they never used and this is where the boys would go and get dressed. It was a nice set up the bar was in the middle with tables set up all around the walls. I could tell it had been shut down for a bit because there was junk sitting everywhere and the carpet was very worn. She was a very nice lady. I really didn't know who she was till they started playing one of her videos. She looked much different than she did in her video. The boys met her the next year during PRIDE too. This year though they got to get to know her a bit more and talk with her.

Once Blane and Bobby got the bar all wired and had been there for about three months the bar owners told them they were going another way with their bar. Once again the boys had to leave. They were playing the POOL on the weekend at this point also. Unfortunately the managers at the POOL still booked wedding receptions on the nights when the managers knew the gay community was going to be there.

One night I overheard a group of Black Americans making some very derogatory racist remarks about the behavior of the gay people there. The comment that stuck out in my head above all else was her calling them … those people. I turned to the lady and said… weren't you all called those people not to long ago. She really didn't have anything else to say. It blew my mind we were just dancing, drinking and having a good time that night like we did all the time and here was a group of people who were letting their attitudes ruin their event. If they wanted to be mad at anyone it should have been the ones who book their reception for that night without telling them so if they wanted to change dates or places they could have.

The Pool was beautiful. It sat on top of a high-rise downtown. As you walked through a softly blue lite hallway this effect was done by hundreds of softly lite blue lights hanging down along the wall as you walked through. The smell of chlorine filled the air. I love the smell of chlorine because it brings back wonderful memories from my time on the beach. It opened up to reveal a water fountain in the middle of the pool with different colored lights shining through it. This made the lights cascade throughout the pool. This setting made for great pictures because it was in this area the boys danced at. There were two bars and one of them was at the end of the pool. The warm breeze blowing through the cabanas and the soft comfortable furniture made me think of the time I was in Miami…all it was missing was the sand. It was great. Allen would also be there with hot men to look at as if you needed more than the dancers. Michael would model for him sometimes. Actually Allen used Wayne to model. When they guys started dancing at the pool was the really the end of Wayne being around. He wanted to do body building competitions and modeling. He danced with Michael a few times at Tree Top but only a few and then just fell of the face of the earth. I loved talking to Allen but he stayed pretty busy when he was there. He had closed his store front and just kept his on-line business going and when he would come to events. Michael loved to dance there. I even got Mr. Glass drunk enough to get out there and dance with Michael. I realize now that I have not explained why we call him Mr. Glass. He has broken every bone in his body. He actually went to smack his dog once and barely hit the table and broke like 4 bones in his hand. Now you can understand why we call him Mr. Glass.

One night Michael and Rick were dancing at Bottom's bar. So the night was going great I was having a good time talking to people and taking pictures. Rick came to me and said this guy was becoming a bother because he wouldn't leave him alone and wasn't tipping. I told him to tell Michael and maybe he could help him. This guy was drinking heavily and towards the end of the night this guy was at the stage of drinking just before you pass out. As the night continued he became very determined and very very friendly by putting his hands all over Rick every time he came out. Michael tried to save him by trading places with him. In a blink of an eye this guy had pulled out Michael's junk and put it in his mouth. I have never seen Michael backtrack so fast. As Michael looked up he saw Blane and Bobby looking at him with big grins on their faces. My only regret of the night was I wish I could have caught Michael's expression on the camera when that guy did that to him because that would have been a perfect picture.

By this time I was very comfortable with going out with my husband and actually had yelled at Scott a few times because he would come and ask me where Michael was and I would tell him each and every time it was not my turn to baby sit. My job became taking pictures full time and drinking. Some night I did a great job others not so much. The quality of the pictures depended on how drunk I got that night. Oh, don't get me wrong, the beginning of the night there were always good pictures but depending on who showed up to talk to me but by the end, well, not so much.

I was still dealing with some issues at home. I hated his clients. They interfered with my family time and our sex life. Michael has never really been interested in sex. He loves sex but just doesn't have to have it. So clients took what time I had and cut it in half. Then you put buddy time in there. You are looking at a smaller percentage. Explaining the difference between a buddy and client is easy. A buddy you want to be with a client is someone who would never get you unless they paid you. I talked about clients before so the client thing is explained. I kind of fixed the buddy cutting into my time because if I'm not getting it then he doesn't get it. I hate doing that but when you are dealing with someone with a low sex drive then you have to figure something out. I will say though when I do get it …. It is so worth it and I don't normally want it for a week.

I hate when he is getting to know a new buddy. Some times that became overwhelming and I would get upset and bothered. I guess you could say I was jealous. All the texts would get on my nerves. It's hard to sit there and watch your husband establish a sexual relationship with someone because he is developing a type of friendship with them. The start of any relationship is full of excitement getting to know someone. Everyone puts on their A game. He was being told he was sexy and people flirted with him. The only person I wanted to flirt with was flirting with someone else. It is hard when attention you want from someone is being given to someone else.

We had been together for a long time now and had been through so much that it wasn't new anymore. We all can understand that but that doesn't mean we don't miss that flirtation we all had at the beginning. Push comes to shove though I knew that whoever he was talking to wasn't getting his heart and that was most important. Having his heart is something I knew I had but that didn't mean I didn't want the other things too. I like the dates and the dirty texts and talking to me like we are getting to know each other even though we have been together forever. We try to keep each other happy by doing little cute things to each other and for each other. Life, kids, jobs, and all the BS that comes up tends to take away from the intimate things we need.

I finally realized I wanted something just for me something nobody else would have. Michael wanted to go out to a bar and hang out with his buddies drinking and dancing. To me that is a date and you don't date toys. I have always told him that if he could find a friend that didn't want to sleep with him than go out and have fun but he can't. He would say it was just hanging out but it sounded like a date to me. I explained he and I had not been out on a date for a year since our last anniversary. I wanted something just for me. I wanted to go out on dates and spend adult time with him. I told him if we could have that then if he wanted to, every so often, go out on what I called a date and what he calls hanging out was fine.

I needed more of something but wasn't sure what. I am not an emotional person but sharing has made things weird. Since his attention is on someone else I needed more soft attention which I was not getting. I needed him to come up behind me and whisper on my neck. I needed to be told more often that I was his one and only. I wanted him to dance in our living room with me and sing. All of these things happened before but now not so much. Oddly enough I didn't need or really want those things before but after all the BS we had gone through and the crap we were still going through I think that I needed that once in a while.

When I get in those moods I tend to hate all things gay…sorry to say that. I think I am aloud I don't always like to share. All the time spent dancing, all the time spent on the computer setting up clients, time spent talking to friends on the computer which always comes around to sex, waiting on someone to answer about getting a client, talking to buddies all these things are gay. More of his life is spent on that side then our side. Most of his time is spent dealing with something on that side.

I did realize something though about the time I was sick of the buddy thing they were usually done talking because he figured out they were not a good fit for him. If they get needy quick or emotional it is a stopper for him. When men get needy, meaning the need to see him or talk all the time or emotional telling him they are only into him or calling him honey or baby, makes them come across to soft for Michael. Michael is done. I will say though I am glad that he takes his time to get to know someone before he hooks up because it keeps out the crazies.

Fun facts that I have observed or have heard my husband say or explain to me. Some men seem to look in a fun house mirror when describe themselves. When you hear the words athletic you think of the body type of Ryan Reynolds or Jake Gylenhaul when you hear someone say they are muscular body builder type you think of the Rock or Vin Desil.... right... everyone can agree with me and you know that. In the gay world some men who are clearly not in those calibers think that they are. We call that the fun house effect.

When Michael is online on his sites you have to type in what you are looking for. Some of the choices are muscular, athletic, jock, swimmer, average and bear are just a few terms you can type in to find someone you are interested. One of my husband's biggest pet peeve is the fun house mirror in men's minds. I have heard him say this time and time again ... And in what fun house mirror are they looking in. My husband likes well-built men who act like men. He has no real need for a bottom, I am his bottom. Oh in case you don't understand that ... all women are bottoms because we don't have an outie. So my husband likes athletic or muscles and when he puts those words into the search and gets some 250 - 300lbs naked old guy with no muscle all fat.... Really what fun house mirror is he looking in.

Michael works really hard to look the way he does. He goes to the gym 4 or 5 times a week he puts forth the effort to look good for me and his jobs. His philosophy is why would he want to get with a guy who doesn't take the time to look the best they can. Also if you say your average then you are not worth his time because you don't think anymore of yourself than that; so why should Michael.

Appearance is a huge aspect in the world especially in the gay world. Nobody is going to approach you in a bar if you don't stand out. That is why in nature the males are more colorful and boisterous. All males are like that so just FYI if you want to get hit on or picked up when you go out … dress to impress. If you don't try your best don't complain on Facebook the next day nobody really feels sorry for you because they know you. You post on Facebook that men are shallow because you couldn't get the hot well-dressed guy you wanted last night or on line when you didn't put your best foot forward. They will never get to know the real you if they can't find you in the sea of beautiful colors.

On line would be the same thing. Don't think just because you have a dirty pick that shows your big belly and junk everyone is going to rush to talk to you.

Another thing I have noticed is some men don't just find one thing and stop. They are constantly looking and if something better comes along they move on. Michael just shakes his head when he is talking to someone and the conversation is going good and then all of a sudden the conversation stops or the replies don't come the way they were and then stop. Michael does not understand why men are always looking for the next best thing. I don't get why someone would give up something they enjoy just to try something else that may not be as good. The grass is not always greener on the other side.

Something that neither one of us understands is why people will post pictures from 20 years ago or pictures that are not even them. This tells me that they don't have much faith in themselves. That someone liking them won't happen and that they don't find themselves attractive. I think this is why they use old pictures or pictures of someone else to try and lure people to them. This is really sad. Trust me when I say nobody is horny enough to come to your house and stay once you open the door and you are not in any way what you looked like on line. Take better pictures, work out and make yourself look better…put forth the effort and you will have better luck getting what you want.

I said all that because Michael hosted an underwear show at Chris's. They were looking for contestants to participate so Michael went out into the crowd to find people before it started. I was shocked to see the crappy underwear people were wearing out to the bar knowing they went to the bar to hook up. I guess their mom never told them the underwear story about always were clean nice underwear out you might be in an accident. I understand men pull their pants and underwear down at the same time but still…. where is the pride in yourself.

So in short … don't blame men for not getting to know what a great person you are when your package doesn't stand out. It is like marketing. You would not keep your job very long if you created packages for a major corporation that you present to the men you are trying to attract at the bar. Straight men are bad about this too. They let themselves go and then bitch because the woman gains weight carrying their kids and because we take care of those kids all day we look worn out. They want us to look like the bombshell they married. Well here is a hint help us take care of the kids. Pay attention to us instead of sports or beer. I think it is bullshit but it is true.

Ok I think it is about time to dive into the breakdown of the gay community of men for a second. Over the years I have learned a great many things by listening to people and have found out one thing. They are the most divided group of people especially within their own group.

Now bears men are usually older and larger heavy or muscular, males who are hairy. There are three subtypes to these; muscular, polar, and sugar. Next we will go with the term cub. A cub is smaller, younger heavier hairy male. There are two subcategories to cubs and they are muscular and sugar cubs. The next one is a wolf which is confused with bears but a wolf is not as hairy, leaner, attractive and sexually aggressive. Characteristically, a wolf is gay male who is semi-hairy, muscular, lean, attractive and sexually aggressive. Ok let's next move on to with an otter. They are a thinner male with hair but usually keep it trimmed with or without beards. There are so many others that I am not going to get in to except to name them; chubs, superchub, pups, bulls, twinks, twunks, gym bunnies, and jocks. Like I said there are so many I can't keep up or understand most of them. Most men cannot even tell who is in what category unless they are an example that fits everything.

You know in high school where everyone was labeled and we hated it. To me it sounds like high school again. I think you should just like people for who they are. Trust me when I say unless you fit in the category they are into or like they don't even give you the time of day. They scoff and turn up their noses. To me this makes men very shallow. I know looks are what gets our attention but just because you like the package doesn't mean what is inside is worth a crap. Ok sorry I will get off my rant now and back to the story ... told you I digress sometimes.

A guy Michael had met on-line got back in contact with him. Once again he was trying to get him back into porn. There was a company that wanted mid-west guys for porn. I am glad that never happened because that is one thing I could not have watched. My opinion of my husband has never changed and I don't think badly of him because he is bi but if I were to see him in a submissive role or with a woman I think I would have a problem with that. I know I would have a problem with the woman. I know me well enough to know that to see my husband in a submissive role or in any way weak would cause us problems. I also know that is not the type of porn he would do so a women being there would not be an issue.

I have always had a problem with weak people. In the past I walked on them. I'm not talking about those who cannot stand up for themselves because those people I protect. Yes that is bad and I feel horrible about that but I want someone to walk and stand beside me not behind me. I know he is a bottom and to know something and to see it is something totally different. He is verse but we agreed that with me being his bottom then if he steps out of the marriage then he needs to be the bottom.

It also is how I know he has sex. It is not soft and sensual sex it is more like hard core. You know the kind where your head is buried in a pillow, drilling you so hard that you feel it for days after and well it is hard to explain but sensual it is not. I am fine with that. I find that type of sex hot.

I should explain that a bit more. Michael is verse but if he is going to be stepping out for sex he needs to be the bottom because he has a bottom at home. I understand he can do things with a toy (his buddy) that he won't do with me because he doesn't want to hurt me but he just needs some self-control. He is married and I understand the need but if you have a bottom then you don't need a bottom. I understand that men are not soft with their bottoms and that is a turn on but I feel that since we agreed that he could step out there needs to be some self-control. So when it comes to a buddy he needs to be the bottom and as far as I know he is.

One night at Tree Top, oh wait I have not described what it looked like. It was a restaurant on one side and a bar on the other. The bar has an upstairs patio that they open for the summer. The décor of the bar is that of the 50's and 60's. There are old movie star pictures hanging up and posters of old movies that are famous. I never really liked the bar because they were not very nice people except for one lady I met there. She was a short firecracker of a girl who was very sweet with brown hair and loved to talk and laugh. I have seen her once or twice at Chris's since I stopped going there but do not run into her very often.

Scott found a new dancer named Arnold, we call him the Canadian. He was something else. That night he brought his girlfriend with him but they didn't last very long. She told him dancing was degrading to which he replied...And you want fries with that isn't. Arnold is tall and lean with a very tone body. He had blonde hair all over a bit more hairy for my taste but because he was blonde it did not stick out. He wasn't a bad dancer but trying to take his picture was like pulling teeth. He is shy and always turns away. I don't know if it is the color of his skin with the lights or what but I can take 100 pictures of him and only 1 will turn out. To this day we are not sure what he likes actually, I think, he just likes sex and whatever strikes his attention is what he goes after.

He began dancing with Michael whenever he could. He had several DUI's so he had no license. When he had a ride or after he got a bike he would dance. I will say he is extremely smart. He is going to school now for engineering and has been on the presidents list a few time. Drinking though is his downfall good story to come later about that.

That year for Pride JR asked Michael and the boys to dance again. Rick, Wayne, Allen, Michael and there was one other one but he didn't last very long so I don't remember his name, danced. They ended up looking like the Village People for one set. This was not planned it just happened. When they figured it out they were on it...switching gear to play up the theme. They turned all sorts of gay. They were hilarious. Imagine seeing them all act out the Y.M.C.A. song although I got to see it backstage. They were a riot. The chemistry between them was just like family. There was a real bond. It is still like that. Michael and I love each and every one of the boys.

This year the venue had put up a barrier about 5 feet away from the stage. It was to keep the people from getting pulled up on stage and throwing money but they still threw money. I found it funny that they did things to prevent people from having a good time. Nothing happened the year before that would be seen as bad or harmful. I think it was a personal choice of the establishment against the gay community but that is just my opinion. I know PRIDE isn't what it started out to be but why bother them when all they want to do is have a good time. That is ok we all had a great time anyway.

Michael called Scott and told him he had a gig at one of the casinos for an event that Blane and Bobby were hosting. Scott had to leave early that night and left Michael and I in charge to make sure things ran smoothly. I had gone that night to take pictures for Michael but it turned into running around making sure things ran smoothly.

People watching is something I love to do and sometimes I do it without realizing it. That night I noticed something that struck me as odd. Everyone that showed was there to have a good time, drink and see a show. This is the odd part the straight people stayed to themselves and just watched from a distant. Not really getting involved or trying to enjoy the event. I wondered why they came if not to have a good time. Why were they being so stand offish?

Everyone else was drinking, dancing and socializing. When I went outside to smoke everyone that was straight were complaining about all the gay people and how they were ruining their night. When the gay people came out they were talking about being excited about the performers and what a good time they were having. One time while I was outside smoking a straight girl asked me for a light and the guy I was talking to tried to light it and she said No SHE can light it. I looked at her and said ... sorry he lite mine I don't have one. We tossed our cigarettes and went back inside. I don't understand why she thought her behavior was ok when clearly it wasn't. Why would they come to a public event and not have a good time. I couldn't believe they were that hung up on the fact gay people were there. The gay people there were not ruining their night they were by acting that way.

There were two performers there that night, Kaci Bataglia and Erica Jane. Erica Jane came out and did a few songs with her entourage dancing with her. Kaci Bataglia didn't have anyone with her. She asked Blane to ask Michael if he and one of the other girls to dance with her. She really only wanted Michael, but that would look odd on the stage just to have one dancer up there with her, so she picked a girl too. It was so cool to know Michael was asked by Kaci Bataglia to dance with her on stage. I could not wait to see him dance with her on stage...what an honor. They were actual performers you heard on the radio. He looked so happy and excited. The last thing he said to me was to tell me to get good pictures and I did.

I got some really good pictures of him and a nice video. You know all the stories you hear about celebrities about only green M&M's and crazy stuff like that. Well Erica Jane wouldn't let her fake toy gun get touched and wanted nobody in her dressing room at all even to let her know it was time to go on. I didn't have to deal with her so for me it was a really fun time.

Michael was so excited. He knew who they were and liked their music. It was a night to remember. Looking back even now I am saying it with a smile. I am so proud of him and all the things he has done over the years. I cannot wait to see what the future holds for him.

One night at my favorite bar I went downstairs to see what was going on. They played Top 40 downstairs. Bill, the DJ upstairs, played good music but some of his stuff was things he liked not everyone else. Bill is a much older man. He keeps his hair extremely short he even goes bald. He is kind of average looking. He can get in a mood sometimes because of everything that gets put on his shoulders. His boyfriend Darrin is a wonderful man too. He also wears his hair really short. Every time I see him in the bar I walk up behind him and scratch his head. He and I talk a bit sometimes and I enjoy his company. Over the years I would say we have become friends. I like Bill too but I do not get the opportunity to talk to him as much because he is always in the DJ booth. I have heard he is going to retire soon. I hope they both still come in because I would miss them both.

Bill has actually told me that he plays what he likes and he didn't care if anyone else liked it. You can see this because there are nights when the dance floor is pretty empty because of the music he plays. This was one of those nights where he was playing what he wanted so I wanted to go downstairs. I was already on my way to being drunk but a guy asked to buy me a shot and I said sure. He and I did a shot together and he ordered three more. From the other side of me I heard a voice say my partner and I like to take a woman home from time to time for us to share. I turned to see this man with a very predatory look on his face … I put down the shot and said no thank you and walked away. It was the first time that I realized that not everyone in there was gay. I know that seams naive but I really did think that I don't know why I thought that because Michael isn't gay but I did.

The next time I was at Chris's I had been told by my husband that I was not allowed downstairs because he can't see me. He was worried that if something were to happen to me he couldn't save me. So me being me what do you think I did … yup I went downstairs anyway. I ran into a guy in a purple shirt, which is what I called him because I can't remember his name.… yes I was drunk again. Anyway, I guess he got my phone and put his number in there that night. He seemed to follow us around that summer because everywhere we went he seemed to be there.

He kept trying to get me to leave Michael because when we were out Michael and I are not married. (We do this because he is working and if people know he is married it will hurt the money he can earn.) I tried to explain to him that he treated me good and loves me but he wouldn't see it or let it go. I finally got angry and told him that if I ever did leave my husband I sure wouldn't date or marry anyone with this glitch. The only reason Michael and I are together is because we have been through so much together.

Scott was getting them a few jobs here and there but nothing really much to talk about. I began going out more when Michael would dance. I enjoyed going out. I went out all of the time when I was single and since we had gotten married we had not been out much. Not much happened at the beginning when I would go out with Michael. I mainly hung out with Mr. Glass and Brent. We were drinking buddies. One night when Michael was dancing his sister and boyfriend came out and hung out with me, Mr. Glass and Brent. They didn't stay long that night because she had to work. She had fun and was very excepting of her brother. We found out a few months later why.

Michael was dancing there again and I had asked Mr. Glass and Brent to come out and hang with me. Brent was the quieter of the two but tonight was not the case. A girl and two guys sat down at a table right in front of where Michael was dancing. I had got up to take pictures and walked over and stood by the table. One of the guys that were sitting there said hi and started a friendly conversation with me when the girl walked back over. She became an instant bitch. This is where this mild mannered gentleman stood up and looked at her and said, "Well her fags are better looking than yours." She was not a happy camper. All I and Mr. Glass could do is laugh. She though, told her group they were leaving and left.

Tonight I learned what a fag hag was. When I found out it made what happened all that more funny. A fag hag is a female that is straight who likes to be a part of all the gay activities and they and go out with their gay friends. Brent was right about one thing mine was way better looking than her's.

That Christmas we went to Tom's. We had heard that the bar was closing. The reasons we heard about the bar closing we not that outlandish considering who they were about. Over the years I have heard some interesting stories about the owner of Tom's but who knows they all just may be that rumors. The only thing that makes me want to believe it is because of who told to me. All we know is that it was closing and having a Christmas party that we were going to.

Now I don't like to gossip but when you hear the same story from many people and they all say the same things then I don't just call it gossip. So people say that Tom's friend was taking liquor from another bar and bringing it back Tom's so that Tom wouldn't have to spend money on liquor. Funny at the same time a friend of Michaels fired a guy for stealing liquor and that same guy started working at Tom's. So I came to my own conclusions and I'm going to let you come to your own conclusions but I know where mine are.

So this was going to be their last Christmas party so Michael and I wanted to go. We invited Michael's sister and her then boyfriend, which nobody liked, to the bar with us. It was a fun night. Tom came out in drag and began the show. One of the special surprises Tom had ordered for the bar was McRibs. That night we took home throw blankets, shot glasses and some other trinkets. It was a lot of fun the only odd thing about the night was the new information we had about Lisa.

During the night Tom, known as Tipsy in drag, went around and asked people questions and jokingly picked on them. When she came to our table she was talking about sexual orientation, I am so glad she skipped over me and went right to Michael. By this time they knew the story about me and Michael. Her skipping over me didn't surprise me. She made the comment about she knew what Michael liked…that wasn't the odd funny part though. The odd funny part is she asked Michael's sister and boyfriend. Their answer was shocking they both said they were bi and liked three ways. Later that night Michael and I talked about their answer. We both knew what the boyfriend was getting out of the deal but had no idea about Lisa. Lisa is a very beautiful girl and the boyfriend ... well not so much. Their relationship lasted longer than we wanted it to but when Lisa told him that she wanted to stop they fought about it and now are not together. Her boyfriend now, though, is a keeper, we really like him. I told Michael though that I thought it was funny because Lisa was adopted but they both were bi. I guess their mom had more influence on them then I thought because that is the only common denominator.

The year started off very slow. Scott wasn't really getting them any work except for the occasional job. This just made money tighter for us as a family. When money got tight that just meant Michael did more clients. I know I have told ya that I didn't look down on Michael for what he did for his family but like I said before it still didn't make me happy.

So far the buddy thing was working out fine. Michael would leave for about two hours and come home and love on me and we would go right back into our life together. For a lack of a better way to say it I give him permission. He wants to make sure I know that he is thankful and that he appreciates me for being understanding. There are some odd things that should be said about how this works out for us.

First, I do give him permission. If I said no then he would lie and cheat and we wouldn't be married. I have asked Michael if he would stop if I asked him to. Michael has always said the same thing to me. He would try his hardest but he would be afraid in the end it wouldn't be enough and he wouldn't want to hurt me again by lying to me. So yes I do give him permission to go and take care of his business. We don't like to call it that but we are married and when you're married then you do give your spouse permission to do things. I know that sounds bad but there is not a better way to say it...I allow...I agree... it all still comes back to me giving permission.

Now a hint for the men who have decided to tell their wives let me give you some advice because this is the way she will see it. You are wrong!!!! Just know that you are wrong and always remember that. You are stepping out on your wife which makes you wrong. Please do not, when you get angry, ever say you are free white and over 21 because you are not free. You are married which makes you not free. The other thing not to say is you're not my momma. These comments will get you punched, slapped or shot at in one case, because we will not hear anything you say after that. We are so mad we are killing you in our mind. Michael has said those things to me and I didn't hear anything he said after that because all I wanted to do was kill him. Needless to say he only said it once ... well seriously once the rest of the time he is just trying to get a rise out of me.

I know that telling your wife or hearing this from your husband will be hard. Just remember you two love each other and it is best to listen to the other person's feelings without being judgmental or condemning. Your husband will be exposed and the wife will be hurt and I mean hurt to the core. Actually heartbroken is a better word. With that there will be a whole range of emotions that will come during that first conversation. It is best to just listen to her and take your verbal beating because remember the first thing...you're in the wrong.

She will not understand why she isn't enough for you. When you try to explain this to her remember she is not bi and doesn't understand the need you have. Even for me I don't fully get it because to me sex is sex and if Michael and I are having sex then that should be good enough. It's better to answer the questions she asks. The best way to approach this subject is the toy scenario. The men are just a toy when you're done playing with them you throw them back in the toy box and forget about them till next time. She is your life and that is something that will never change.

The first buddy I ever met, Juan, well you can't really call him a buddy, because buddy implies that you hook up often and they didn't. Juan is a very nice guy. He is a cutie and so sweet. He came over here from Cuba where he was married and still is but she is still there. He can never go back to Cuba because they kill gay people even today. How sad is that. Here is this really nice man who is very passionate and caring and Cuba would kill him if they found out he was gay.

He actually invited Michael and me over for dinner one night. I just couldn't go and eat on a table or sit on a couch where he had my husband. Juan made some comments to Michael that I didn't like. I'm sure you all are thinking the same thing so I will tell ya. He asked Michael if he really loved me then why was he here with him. Yes Michael liked him as a friend but as for the sex he was just a toy. Michael could hang out and talk with friends without sex but because he was having sex with him that part he was just a toy. Michael isn't that cold but that is the feeling behind the sex Michael has with others. Michael separate the 2 emotions, the emotions you have towards friends and the non-emotion you have towards someone you are just having sex with. With me there is no separation we love each other and we love each other together during sex.

I don't hold it against Juan for asking the question. Most people don't understand how things are. They just pass judgment and jump to conclusions without ever knowing either of us. I guess I could have been petty and told Michael to not talk to him or have sex with him but then I wouldn't have a great friend with a heart of gold. It would be petty too.... just because someone doesn't understand and asks questions that doesn't mean you have to be angry or mean to them. If I had done that I would be as bad as everyone else who judges people without knowing them.

Over the years I have listened and watched the gay men I know. One thing I found is they wanted a relationship with someone they could love. Listening to them though...what they wanted does not exist in men. Women are the only creatures on the planet to fill the void. Men want someone to love and to love them. They want a partner. They want someone to take care of ... to protect. They want someone to protect and to be soft with. Men want to be babied and pampered. Problem is most men can't let another man do this and they can't act this way towards another man and be comfortable with it forever. Their masculinity won't let them. They don't see other men as something they should have to take care of or protect and they don't want to appear weak. Men are not raised that way unless it is towards a woman. Men are men and are not very forthcoming with their feeling. They are the ones who take care of and fix things. Boys are all taught to be the little man and take care of mommy while daddy is away. I have noticed that men have no respect for other men who are considered weak. Even the weak males don't like what they consider weak.

Men can only accept this behavior from a woman. Men tolerate other men and become comfortable. They form a bond and in that bond they 'fall in love'. The only way for 2 men to be happy together is to find someone's tolerance level the same as theirs and is ok with being the 'female' sometimes. Monogamy still though is not something they conform to. I have not met one couple who are still physically attractive who are monogamous. Another thing I have found is that a lot of gay couples rush into saying I love you and I am not sure why. They are maybe reaching for accepting and belonging behavior like they saw between adults when they were growing up. This is just a shot in the dark and blind thinking but then this is all my opinions and things I have experienced.

I have found from talking and listening to men that when men get to old to go out and get what they want they settle for what they have and some even pay for what they want. A real relationship is not just sex but joining together thru it all...good and bad. Not letting life get in the way. Most gay couples don't use one bank account. When you start out and continue a relationship separate then that is what you will have as time goes on...a separate relationship. Now I get it if they are doing this to protect the other half because of the family behaviors if one dies. I so do not agree with the family swooping in and taking everything if they had disowned them for being gay. I feel the courts should stop this behavior. This is my opinion based on what I've seen and what people have said.

I should tell you about one of my other rules. I didn't want Michael to hook up with any black guys. I know that it is stereo-typical but I didn't want him hooking up with any black men because they sleep around a lot and I didn't want that for my husband. The ones that I have met and of course seen on T.V. have all cheated on their wives and could not be trusted. This is bad I understand but it is the way I felt. I told you that to tell you about my husband's next buddy.

The next buddy I met I call my 'other husband' or TeddyBear. He is a very handsome, around 6', tight curly haired although sometimes he keeps it very short, which I like better, and the nicest dark chocolate color skin. He is the most beautiful souled man that would do anything for the family and I mean the whole family. I remember the first night I met him. He came out to watch Michael dance. When Michael brought him over to meet me he was nervous. I knew we were going to be friends just by his eyes and smile. I could tell he had a gentle soul...a heart of gold. He was very warm and inviting in the way he talked and interacted with Michael and I. Michael had to get back up and dance but he and I talked like we had been friends forever. He said a few things out loud that he probably wished I did not hear but I loved the honesty in front of me. He talked about Michael like a man should, in my opinion. Over time I knew that he came to care about Michael very much but I was ok with it because he wasn't making me uncomfortable at the same time.

Our friendship has continued to this day. I am very thankful that I met him. He will come out and we will dance with each other and I love it. Well you have to make him drink a few shots before he will dance but that is not hard to do. We laughed and talked most of the night that night. When he laughs you have to smile. He is perfect and I love him.

He told Michael later that he really enjoyed meeting me. I am so glad he did or I would have nobody to run away with. We now text each other and plan Michaels death and our runaway plans. He has my heart and always will.

That Halloween Michael had come up with a great idea for a Halloween costume. He put a twist on the Jack of Hearts. He had bought this sort of top hat with card shapes on each side. He wore this with his black leather pants and an older style vest. We found what we call John Lennon glasses you know those small round thin framed glasses. Everyone loved it. He won the Halloween costume party that night at Tree Top. There were some other wonderful costumes. Three drag queens dressed up as the witches from Wizard of Oz and it was very well done. There was another guy there who made an excellent Elton John.

Some of the other costumes were amazing. I never realize it but Halloween is like the gay Christmas. It is their favorite holiday. Everyone goes all out for it. There costumes are well thought out and many of them are elaborate in design. I was Athena the goddess of war. I didn't think hard on mine. I like Halloween but had never experienced anything like this. Everywhere you looked people looked amazing. I had a lot of fun that year.

It was during this time that I met one of my favorite dancers, Fernando. He had been in the United States for a very long time from Mexico. A cute little shit if I ever saw one. He is one of my favorite of all the dancers. His English was not that good but good enough. He was always very quiet but always made me smile. He always showed me honest affection it was never fake and you could tell. I never really knew much about him till later when he also started working for me at the gas station I ran. One day out of the blue we found out he was married and had been married since we met him. The more I got to know him the better I liked him. You will hear more about him later as I learned it. Now Rick had some competition because they both were wonderful.

One night at Flexx Scott had to leave so he left Michael in charge of the boys. He was supposed to make sure they got paid and keep his money for him. The night went well the boys showed up and everyone enjoyed seeing them. Michael met Maria a lady that told him she wanted to put together a strip group and wanted him to be part of it. At the end of the night the bar owner came in and paid the boys but told Michael that he wasn't paying Scott because he had not been there all night.

I agreed with Michael about that being petty. Scott did what he was supposed to do. Scott was supposed to make sure the bar had dancers for the night. They were there on time and danced the whole night like they were supposed to do. He was always there but his job had changed his hours and was making him work longer and he couldn't be there. Scott usually sat up with the DJ's and talked or was on his phone or computer but he was there. The bar only paid him $25 so I'm not sure why, just because he wasn't there but did his job, they didn't pay him. After all the dance gigs Scott had gotten for the guys it was now over.

So when the bar didn't pay Scott he dropped off the face of the earth. We tried calling and texting but never heard back from him. When we would go out we would ask everyone if they had heard from him and nobody had. Michael talked to people on Facebook and still nobody had seen him. To this day we still have not heard from him. I miss Scott even though we were not close and he never really talked to me I still miss him and hope that everything is ok.

CHAPTER 10

Michael and the boys sat for several months with nothing. The lady Michael had met got in contact with him about a strip gig. Michael talked to the boys and they were all in. The first time they danced for Maria we ended up in this little hole in the wall Mexican bar. I had invited Chuck and Jeff to go with me and hang out. I had not seen them in a while and I had missed them.

She used all of the boys and one of her own. Michael thought he was hot. I though he was not so hot defiantly not my type. When it comes to the average person Michael and I don't normally agree. What I find attractive he doesn't and vice versa. The boys did great that night. Chuck and I sat and joked about the place. I didn't go to the bathroom after I heard about the boy's bathroom.

One of Michael's clients came too and sat with us. I find it funny because when the clients met me they have no idea I know anything. I am not sure why they would think that because of where they met me and they know I know about what he does. I think it might be a case of denial but it doesn't matter because even what I know doesn't change what I think about them or how I treat them. I don't always know details but that is because I don't care…well sometimes he tells me things about people I would have never thought they liked. In all reality I don't care… to each their own. He was a very nice guy. We all sat around talking and had a very good night.

They did about 4 shows for her each one of them was about the same. Some little bar in some random spot full of the Latin community. She was an odd person. I am not sure why she didn't like me I was always nice to her but she would walk right past me and never even acknowledge my presence. I always wonder what people's motives are when they act like that. I don't understand, not that I really lose sleep, but I do still wonder.

As always the boys did great. She had another guy join the strip group. He was an odd guy. He humped everything including the floor. I thought our boys were great and so did everyone else. During this time Michael began to talk to Chris's about the boys dancing there. The story about why the boys were not dancing at Chris's was between Scott and people at Chris's. The truth will never be known whether it was over jealousy or something else but either way I have no idea why they didn't dance there. All I knew is Chris's felt they didn't need to hire dancers. They had guys dancing but they were not very attractive and worked for drinks and tips.

Let me explain something … you know the old saying "You get what you pay for" well that is what was dancing at Chris's. They were twinks. The explanation of that word I had gotten wrong forever. I figured because every time I heard the term there was this small framed, female acting, over the top acting gay man. So easy to say that is what I thought the word meant. Twinks are small framed skinny men. Some twinks are just called that because of their body types. Others are called that because of what I call the total package which was the meaning I thought was right. Anyway Chris's dancers were what I called twinks. They all just stood there and stick out their but and maybe weighed 100lbs. This is not what men want to fantasize about and watch dance.

So far I have noticed a fatal flaw with bar owners. They hire what they like. What they find attractive even if the general masses do not find them attractive. They do not understand that there business could grow if they didn't use these philosophy. Also I have noticed friendship and business do not mix. That will also hurt your business. When you let someone do whatever because you are friends that is not smart business practices. Allowing your friends to dictate how you run your business in not very smart. They are not doing what will bring in your money then what is the point of having them there. You will understand what I mean later because this happened at Chris's.

Michael began to talk to JR about PRIDE again. The street blast was held outside of a bar that had only been open for a short time. This was the year Pride went to crap. The last two Prides Michael had done were good…the first one was the best but the second one was still good but this one was not really that good. It was not advertised really at all and there was no reason for anyone to show up. Michael had started calling the group The Boyz. One of the bars the Boyz danced at had agreed to be the main drive and planner for Pride and backed out at the last minute leaving the rest of the community to scramble to make their own Pride events. I will say that if money is collected all year for pride I have no clue why it was a scramble unless all the money was given to the bar that backed out and they kept it. I would have to imagine that a lot of money is collected over the year but they really did nothing to show for it. This is sad in my opinion because it discourages people from getting involved. Most people do not even know when PRIDE is…now that is sad. Michael and I thought and talked to Colten Ford; he is an internationally known porn star and singer, about doing it but couldn't get any details because we were not in charge of anything. We asked Chris's but they were not interested in bringing him in not to blame them because we couldn't get all the information because of his agent. Not one person really knew what was going on. This is according to all the stories I have been told by several people.

Michael had bought me a camera for Mother's Day and I was excited to try it out. I had been going out as often as I could and take pictures but now I had a better camera to take pictures with. I ran into a friend of ours at PRIDE that night. Chuck had gone out that night to see some of his friends. I had met a few of them at his Christmas party. We didn't talk for long because I had to take pictures.

JR, as always, rocked the stage. Pepper Mashay came to that PRIDE to perform on stage. The drag queen that was hosting was really long winded and slightly odd. I had met her the night we met Maria and found him and his boyfriend a bit off. The impression I got was they like to preach and talk about things but their heart was not in it. I'm not sure what it was I just got an odd vibe from both of them.

PRIDE was the first time the "Boyz" were announced to the world. It was official Michael had created the Boyz. Everyone laughed at him but they don't laugh any more. The group is the only group around that catered to the gay community because all the guys in the group were gay or bi. Finally the gay community had dancers just for them. Oddly enough you would think that this would set them apart. All the dancers are gay or bi and they cater to the gay community but the gay community would rather pay money for other dance groups who shun them and only will pay attention to the women. I find this odd. I would have thought that the "BOYZ" would have been a huge thing but here in their hometown they were not…ODD.

Odd thing about that is the way some people treat them. I guess I should say some of the people who want to hire them. With all the stuff they have done and the way they perform is well worth the money you spend on them. They will give you one hell of a show. In the gay community they all want something for free. I do not understand that. Drag queens will work just for tips and they do not get that much. You would think because the Boyz are there for them they would be excited and pay them. They pay for other strip groups, like I said, that do not let men touch them but our group doesn't care. I know a straight club would never ask Thunder From Down Under to dance and strip just for a portion of the door then why do gay bars think our Boyz should?

One of the first things Michael had to get the Boyz to understand was that if you wanted to be taken seriously then you needed to take yourself that way. He told them that if anyone wanted them to dance they should have them go through him. Michael did this for many reasons: over exposure and knowing who he had for what. It was coming together.

As usual PRIDE ran on gay time. With the drag queen rambling on when she was on stage and all their and other drag queens stuff everywhere backstage. The Boyz had to get dressed in the street because there was no room. Nothing started when it was supposed to. The Boyz were going to do 3 outfit changes that night but because of the delays and talking they only went on twice. The Boyz spent their time taking to the crowd and taking pictures. Rick did a competition with one of the other girl dancers they hired. Each one of them had to see how long they could do a hand-stand then go into a split and a flip landing on their feet … Rick won of course. The Boyz had to get out of there by a certain time because they had been invited to dance at Chris's. This was the beginning of a very beneficial agreement between the Boyz and Chris's. I really didn't get to talk to JR and Brian that night because of the show but I would get to talk to JR at a later time.

Now we were excited because the bar we had been trying to get into had hired the Boyz to dance that night for Pride. So after the stage show we headed over to Chris's. When the crowd saw them walk in everyone became very excited. Everyone wanted to talk to them. It was like someone famous had walked into the room. The Boyz went over very well. The bar heard from that night on that they wanted to see the Boyz. They were done with the people the bar had been using they wanted the Boyz.

This act really pushed Michael in to the lime light. The rest of the dancers found out that they began to have a following. Over the years they have become celebrities in their own right. I have created a like page on social media and a website. The fan page has over 3,000 followers. The fans love the video's I make and the pictures I take. Oddly though I am not focused on, this is a good thing because I am not the one who should be focused on. I am still a fly on the wall. I have a few people come up and say they love the pictures I take and to keep it up but the focus is on the Boyz where it should be. So a quick Thank You to all the followers they have. Without your love and support we would not be where we are today. It has become a privilege to be picked to dance with the Boyz. It's all odd and sort of funny that something that started out as a hobby would grow to where it is today. I'm getting ahead of myself so let me go back to the story.

Doors began to open up for the Boyz. Private parties, party bus opportunities, bachelorette parties, pool parties, you name it they began to be asked to be involved in it. Some people just wanted them to come to parties they were throwing just to make the party look better. To serve drinks to people in their underwear or chip ice at a fund raiser the Boyz were ready for it all. There was someone to fit all the needs that were coming their way.

Michael now spent even more time on the computer. He also now wanted to go out more by himself to hang out at the bar. I knew he needed to so he has…. not as much as he should. It just brought up issues between us and the trust I still didn't have. It was coming back but not quit there. Another issue I had was because we never really got to go out and have husband and wife time. The only times I knew for sure we would go out was for our anniversary/my birthday and that was because they were two days apart. I really looked forward to our night and nights out. I wanted focus just on me. It seemed he was being pulled to the other side more and more. Everything he seemed to concentrate on was on that side. Everything that makes him get excited is on that side. I understand his thinking now but I didn't understand it then. One of the discussions we always had was about time. Computer time, dancing time, clients, and his once or so a month buddy left me little time with my husband or him with the family... I just wanted him.

I understood people were still unsure of the wife thing. It has gotten better over time. Now I hear them say I am just one of the boys. So Michael out by himself helped the group but that wasn't the only reason he was going out. It was nice for him to have something I never got. He wanted time out away from me and the family to have fun. I wanted time out away from the kids with my husband. There is where the dilemma lies.

I did a lot of running around and doing the things I wanted to do before I had kids. I explored and experienced things that I wanted to do when I was single and now that I am not some of those things are not something I can do. I cannot just pick up and do anything I want to do because I am a mother and a wife. When you are single that is the time to be free not once you settle down. I understand time away with friends but there is a different definition of friends in my book.

He always said he needed time out with his friends. He and I have a different definition of friends. Like I have said before he could go out with a friend if he could show me one 'friend' that didn't want to sleep with him. I explained if I went out with my friends the thought of sleeping with me would never cross their minds. These types of arguments happened when he would get frustrated. The argument never went anywhere. It is hard for either of us to fully see the others side.

The Boys were invited to do a fashion show for Allen to raise money for Latino Pride. It was at a waste of a bar that the last PRIDE had been held in front of. The bar has great potential the set up was in sort of a U shape. The longer bar is on the right side of the U and a smaller bar was in the middle of the U. There was an area where they had a big stage area towards the back and right of the bar. Sadly when the owner is just playing bar it isn't going to go anywhere. All but two of The Boyz participated in the show. Little did we know that two future members of Boys were in the fashion show too.

This being really the first time I had been to the bar I can say I was not impressed. There were not that many people there and the staff was ok, but like I said they were just playing bar. I will say by now I had already made up my mind on my favorite bar which was Chris's but I still had a good night. We left after the fashion show and went to Chris's. Were we had a ball.

By this time people had started talking to me at Chris's bar it was nice. Blake and I had really begun to develop our friendship. The people in the bar had gotten used to me being there. Some of the people there began to talk to me and I was finding my little corner of the bar. I now began to sit at Blake's bar and talk to him off and on all night.

One night Michael was dancing at Chris's. A gentleman came up to Michael and was trying to talk to him about getting dancers to come to their club. Michael sent him over to me where we discussed the Boyz a bit more. We did not talk that much that night but I did get the information I needed to give Michael. All he said was that he ran a quiet little bar that he wanted Michael and Rick to dance at. He wanted us to contact him about a date that he had given us.

We were excited. This was going to be our first out of town gig. The guy had seen the Boyz and wanted them to come to their bar this was kick ass. This was our 1st real gig for the Boyz we were now a group. I mean we were not just some guys who got together and danced at clubs where they live we were being invited out of town.

This also began our road trips. Now the ride to our gigs are filled with lots of conversation and laughter. The trip back is always quiet and everyone is ready to be home. During this trip Rick wanted to stop on the way back every time we passed water and try to find snakes. He loves snakes. We never stopped that is for sure I didn't want a snake in the car. If we ever sit down again the stories I can tell you about the road trips. We all have so much fun talking, drinking and laughing. The road trip and breakfast have become our favorite time out.

They put us up in a beautiful hotel. This was a 2 part hotel room with a bathroom to die for. On one half of the room was like a living area with 2 chairs and even a table to eat at. On the other side were 2 big and soft beds with a long desk and a very large mirror on the wall. Rick went with Michael and me. Remember when I said Rick was a free spirit well I meant it because from the time he walked in the door he was naked. You know he never made me feel uncomfortable though.

That night at the club the Boys were gogo dancers. The bar was very nice. It had more seating area than a dance floor. The bar I thought felt and looked more like an up-scale bar not really a night club. You know a bar that people go to sit and talk not really dance. They served good food there and the bar tender that was there for us was really nice. The people there were, well, let's just say, were strange.

I have never seen so many odd people in my life. I mean just weird people. They all acted as if they had never seen a gogo dancer before. After most of them were drunk they began to come up. It was an odd ritual to watch. A bar that time forgot well at least the people in the bar. A guy walked up to me and began to hit on me. I told him no many times but he wouldn't take no for an answer. I actually had to grab his private parts and tell him to back off before he left me alone. There was another girl who got so drunk she threw up all over the floor right where she was sitting. The odd thing was they all just sat there around her and the mess. It was like it wasn't even there.

I was never so happy to leave that bar in my life. The Boys made pretty good money and went over very well and everyone loved them but the money was not what we expected. After the gig Michael found out from talking with the owners they wanted more than just to pay them in money. Michael and Rick just wanted to go back to the hotel room and go to sleep. This didn't sit well with the owner because they became a bit upset with Michael and Rick.

I guess we never got a call back from the owners because the Boyz didn't put out for them. We all figured that because of his actions. It blows my mind that people expect that kind of thing to happen just because they gave you a job. The owners felt that they should be entitled just because they hired them to dance. I was not happy that they saw The Boyz as toys and not dancers. Some people are very shallow.

This was the first of many things to come for the Boyz. Michael knew all the dancers and they knew him. We were like a family. We are family. I think of all the dancers like my brothers. One of the most frequent questions I get asked by everyone is who is the biggest? Well, I'm here to say for the world to hear…I don't look…they are like my brothers and I don't care to look. I am happy with Michael I don't need to look or care to.

The Boyz, Michael, the Canadian, Rick, and Fernando were the group to call. Not only were they hot but they all were very well liked by everyone. That is one of the biggest attractions they have is how friendly they are.

All of the dancers are bi or gay and they will talk to and dance for anyone. This is not something you get with other male groups. Most of those men are straight and won't show anyone attention but women but the Boyz will show everyone even the men a good time.

They began to dance for Blane and Bobby at Tree Tops on a regular basis. It was good money and they had fun. You would figure the fun came from all the attention they get when they are up on the box but that is only a small part of it. They all like to dance and entertain people. When they see the crowd having a good time they know they are doing a good job. Michael loves to dance and because he can do it in his underwear it makes it even better. The money is the next part but I will explain that in a bit more detail later.

I invited Chuck down to the bar to hang out and chat. I enjoyed hanging out with Chuck even though a few times he left me for something a bit more entertaining … a man. It seemed everyone there but a select few were bitter and mean older bears.

The owners of Tree Top started Bear Bust to help their business. It was a good idea that they turned into something not so on the up and up. This brings up another observation of mine because the event turned into a place for pompous, arrogant, bitter old bears who won't tip unless you let them pretty much do what they wanted to do to you. I know I broke down some of the categories earlier in the book and if you understand them or can identify them you are better than me. So I don't understand why they act that way. Maybe it is because bears in nature act that way. There are more similarities between male bears and what I have seen from gay male bears. Now I am not saying they are all like that but the ones I have met are so I will let you figure out the similarities if you ever met one.

I don't understand men when it comes to men's attitudes. Some feel like the world belongs to them. I know that Michael and I have talked about his attitude towards me and the kids because of how he acts on his bi side. I think it is because when you get to pick and choose what you want all the time and not have to deal with anything else it does change your perspective. On the gay side you can pick through everyone because, at least for Michael, they are just a toy and when you don't have to deal with the everyday stuff then you get an altered sense of perception.

Sense Michael and I have been married I have figured out over time that a marriage is broke down into different parts. You are supposed to truly love the one your with. You know when you look at the other and for no reason you smile. When you think about them and smile for no reason just because you were thinking about them or just because they make you feel all warm and fuzzy. The part of love where you would kill for them and never let anyone or anything hurt them in any way because of how you feel. This is the truest part of love especially when you get these feelings even after you have been together for as long as we have.

I know I have said this before but unfortunately there is the bla time. I call it this because it is when you deal with all the BS stuff like the every mundane stuff, the down time. You know when you are dealing with bills, kids arguing or making them clean their room, jobs, and the everyday crap stuff that nobody is happy about. The next part is intimate time…this is the closeness between two people, the long talks when it is just you and them, the cuddling, holding hands, going out when attention is completely on each other. The last part is sexual…this is the open lines of communication about what you like and don't like about sex and the act of sex itself. Each one of these is vital to a healthy relationship. If you do not have all these things in your marriage then you are really missing out. If you have more of one of these more than the others it alters the way you look at things.

This bar seemed to be full of men that just couldn't get things together. They were more like dictators. Michael didn't want the Boyz to get a slutty reputation and was very happy not to dance there anymore. Rumors spread like wild fire about the owners of Tree Top taking people in the back room for a little bit of fun during the events. You know what I think … to each their own I guess. The money they got when they gogo'd was not good enough to get that type of reputation.

Our marriage was running smoothly. We were going out on date nights. Michael was having buddy time. It was nice having my husband back. No he was still doing clients but not as much because he had gotten a job at a retail store. It was hard for him to run the group though because he couldn't have his phone on him while he was at work. This made it hard for Michael because none of the other dancers were real quick about getting back with him. They missed out on opportunities because Michael wouldn't get an answer from them soon enough. Sometimes it would take a day or so before anyone would text him back. One problem Michael had was…how could he get the world to take the group serious if the guys didn't? This group is not just a hobby for Michael he wants this to be his and their full time job. Things were picking up for the group so there was a lot of information he needed to share with the Boyz.

They were becoming a main stay at Chris's. Although getting information from the DJ was like pulling teeth though. He would text Michael sometimes Friday and tell him that he wanted dancers that night or Saturday night. This didn't leave much time to get people together. Most of the guys would have plans if they didn't hear from Michael by Wednesday. Michael tried his best every time to get them dancers but he was getting tired of all the run around. Nothing seemed to be organized when it came to the entertainment for the bar. I noticed the same drag show went on the only change happened because of a holiday or because of new people in the show. These were mainly straight girls who were getting married and their whoa hoo girls in their parties. You know the girls that yell out trying to get everyone's attention.

I actually heard a woman tell the bartender that their drinks should be half price because she was getting married. Let me explain why that is wrong. You are in a gay bar where they do not have the option of getting married even if they wanted to. Not only are you loud and making an ass of yourself but you are acting the same way you do in a straight club and men may find that cute but in a gay bar they find it tacky. You want to come in fine…drink have a good time but don't make an ass of yourself.

Now at this time Michael was still hooking up with Teddy, my other husband, in case you forgot. He would go out and drink and hang out with me when Michael danced. Michael asked me if he could have more time on one of the nights they were going to have buddy time. I liked Teddy and Michael and I was in a good place so when he asked I said sure. I was going to bed anyway because I was tired so it was not a big deal. All I told him was not to be gone forever. They usually had about two hours so I said a couple more would be fine. Now for those of you that can do math you understand that if someone is gone 2 hours and someone says a couple more … 2+2=4 … right. Well I guess Michael flunked math in school.

Well his first time out with extra time turned into 6 hours. I was pissed. I will never understand why Michael does some of the things he does. To me it always comes back to the lack of respect. I will never understand that. After all the things I have put up with I'm not sure why he would take advantage. Now there is always a wonderful explanation as to why he was late or whatever the issue is but all I hear is BLA BLA BLA.

After all the calls and texts he finally texted back and of course said he was sorry and he would be right home. His excuse for it taking another hour and ½ was that he spent time getting my "other husband" up and around which took 40 minutes because he didn't want him to know "his mommy would be mad". Michael is one that doesn't like for everyone to know his business. In our situation I am not his mommy but he is NOT single. There are "time limits" on time spent outside the marriage. I feel that I cannot be expected to just sit home and let him just do whatever he wants.

There have been things that he has done that have come to bite him in the ass over the years because of the choices he has made. You have already read some of them and there are more so just wait. Needless to say it didn't have much to do with the time it was because he didn't call and let me know that he was going to be gone that long. I have a thing with people dying. What if he was dead in a crash and I wouldn't know. I figure that comes from the twins and our other baby but it doesn't matter it is disrespectful to make people worry. I called but he didn't answer which made it worse. He is the king of coincidence because if it is going to happen it will happen to him.

Michael is an odd duck but smart. See when Michael gets a buddy he really likes he sticks with him. My 'other husband' and Michael developed a close friendship. Michael began to see behaviors from Teddy, 'my other husband', that appeared that he wanted more than just friends. This didn't bother me because I knew that Teddy would have never done anything to try and break up my marriage. He was, as happy as you could be, being in the spot he was in. Teddy would have never made things difficult for Michael in any way when it came to his feelings. One night Michael sat and talked to Teddy about just that. Teddy understood his place in our lives and in our hearts where he will always stay. Teddy always made time for me too. I know this sounds strange but when you are open and honest especially with me I respect you for it. Teddy honestly cared about me and my feelings and made sure I knew that. He included me in everything except what physically happened between him and Michael. That is why still to this day he is my favorite.

There is a place sort of like a boy club where men can meet up and hook up all in the same place. You have to be a member of the club and the way they do this is they have to check all your profiles to make sure you are who you say you are. This is for their protection as well as the people who come in there. You have to be buzzed in through 2 doors before you even get to where the main part is. It has a store beneath it maybe as a cover I don't know. Michael would take buddies and clients there to hook up when they didn't have a place. One day when Michael and Teddy were having buddy time they met Felipe. After Michael and Teddy got done with their time together Michael went out to smoke and make his rounds wearing nothing but a towel. He saw Felipe in the same attire rounding the corner and Felipe saw him too because Felipe watched him as he rounded the corner. Michael went back and told Teddy about what he had seen and told him what way he went because Teddy had asked. Teddy headed out and Michael followed. As they got down the hall Michael stopped to go to the bathroom when Felipe started down the hall. Teddy had gone back in the room when Michael saw Felipe so he stopped in the doorway and gave him a look and Felipe slowed down. Teddy came out and started talking to him. While Teddy was talking to him they found out that Felipe lived about 40 minutes away and that he was bi like Michael. After the conversation Teddy got his number because he thought that Felipe was interesting and maybe they could hang out sometime. When Michael came home he told me that he had met this attractive man that he and Teddy had talked to and he seemed very interesting.

About 2 weeks later Teddy had been talking to Felipe and wanted to hang out with him. He texted Michael and explained that he didn't think Felipe was comfortable with just going out with him. Michael told Teddy that he didn't think he could because he and Teddy had just been out 2 weeks before that. Teddy kept asking Michael to just ask and see. Teddy was telling Felipe that he didn't think Michael could go so Felipe began to back out of going out with Teddy. Michael finally asked me if he could go out and hang out with them. Now we had not been out on a date in a while so that we could spend husband and wife time together and he had just been out 2 weeks ago with Teddy so I was not to happy with him going out to hang out. This actually sparked a very intense conversation that lasted until I gave in and just said yes. Mainly because we were not getting anywhere and I liked Teddy and I didn't want to take it out on Teddy. Michael texted Teddy and told him he could go and began to get ready. Teddy texted Felipe and now Felipe was all for it. Felipe sudden change in attitude about going out pissed Teddy off because he realized Felipe had no interest in him just in Michael. So Teddy texted Michael and told him he wasn't going and gave Michael Felipe's number. Michael was dead set on going out now because of our argument so he talked to Felipe and told him to just meet at the place where they had met…the bathhouse. So that they could talk about what to do next because that was the only place Michael could think of to meet that Felipe would be comfortable with.

Now when Michael left I was under the impression it was going to be the 3 of them. Now years later I found out the real story and that they met at the bathhouse…went in…and hooked up before going to a little restaurant to talk. Now yes it didn't change anything talking in today's time line for Michael and I but that the lack of respect and Michael thinking only about himself still strikes a nerve and pisses me off when I find out things… there are others in here but I am glad I didn't know back then or I wouldn't be here. Michael says this is why he doesn't tell me stuff but I think he just shouldn't do shit that he knows slaps me in the face.

Michael and Felipe talked all that next week and Felipe mentioned that he would like to see him dance. Michael told him he was dancing that weekend. Felipe told Michael he didn't think that he could come to a gay bar and Michael pointed out that they had met at a bathhouse in a towel.

Felipe was a very closeted bi guy. He had only been with 2 guys and one of them they didn't have full blown sex. He seemed to be someone not comfortable in his own skin. He had a guy that he was kind of hooking up with but he was the one that was not full on sex. So when he and Michael met he stopped seeing the other buy. This is why it was such a big deal for Felipe to come to Chris's to see Michael dance.

The interest Michael showed in Felipe posed a slight issue for Michael. While there was no relationship rule with Teddy there was a kind of understanding between the two of them. Michael told me that there was something off about Felipe but that was a nice looking and had a decent body and enjoyed talking to him and wanted to continue to see him. I told him I didn't know what to tell him.

The next time Michael danced Teddy and Felipe were at Chris's. This was the first time I met Felipe. I noticed a bit of tension between them but didn't understand why. Now I know that it was because Michael had told Teddy that they had hooked up when Teddy didn't go out with them. Teddy and Felipe had not talked to each other since that night. Teddy was making things uncomfortable for Felipe because after he had a few drinks he began talking to Felipe about what a nice ass Michael had and saying what a good fuck Michael was other more dirty things that make me think of a soap opera. Felipe was getting pissed at Teddy.

I must have been talking to Blake because I never even saw them really having anything to do with each other. I thought the night was great because Teddy and I were our normal selves. We did some shots and because Teddy is such a lightweight after only 3 drinks he becomes a social butterfly and wonders around the bar talking to everyone. It wasn't soon until Teddy was off making his rounds and left me alone with Felipe. I agreed with Michael that there was something off about Felipe. I decided to find out what it was. I knew he wasn't as young as what he said but that is not what I picked up on. There was something else. You couldn't be that naïve and be as old as what he looked. I figured in time I would figure it out. All in all I liked him and he had what seemed to be an amazing heart.

Now around this time The Boyz had just finished their first male revue show. They had gotten this gig because one night when Michael was dancing at Chris's one of Michael's followers told him about a club where he lived. He loved what he saw from the Boyz and knew the Boyz would go over well. Michael talked to him and found out that there weren't any real gay bars around. They all had shut down and most of the gay people were now going to other bars in town. He told Michael that a group like theirs had never been done and really wanted to bring them to his home town. He knew the owner of a bar and told Michael that he would talk to him. It wasn't very long before the owner contacted Michael on Facebook with a number and told him to give him a call.

Michael called him and book his first male review show at Rumors. The Boyz began preparing for the show. Michael began to plan out a group routine for the show. I never realized what all had to go into a male review show. First you have to get all the music downloaded to one place. You wouldn't think that would be hard but waiting for everyone to get Michael there music seems to be a nightmare. Everyone seems to send all the music the night before the show. Next was picking who goes where and does what. This is another hard thing to do because everyone is at different places with their dancing and this was the first show and you want it to go over well. The only thing Michael had to go on is what he remembered from when he was 19 or 20 when the bar he worked out would hire men to do a revue show.

You want the best to go with you so they will call you back. This also works for networking. If someone attends the show and likes what they see then they may hire you or tell others about you. There are the outfits the guys will wear. You have to think about different outfits and all the underwear you have to take because you just can't wear tighty whities. Michael set his shows up with flare. Every detail was thought about and for him that meant every outfit, song, what he was going to say ... everything had to be planned out. It finally came together and we hit the road.

Every show has their minor setbacks and this one was no different. People forgot part of their gear, make-up and part of the opening number. Nervous plays a part in the set back too and if you have never performed then you wouldn't understand. You know you never really know people until you travel with them. That trip we came up with the game we call who gets the Ho hat. You get this by your behavior during the road trip, what you do during the show and the meal after the show. It isn't who slept with who it is more about over all actions and things that are said. Rick got the hat this time. He came up to me all excited and told me to come with him because he wanted a picture. When I got there Rick bent over this guy and pulled out this guy's junk and wanted a picture. I still have the picture in the vault. Not to mention while he was talking to someone and another person was eating his ass. Rick never missed a beat in the conversation he was having. I still just smile and shake my head.

There is a high you get after the show is over. The adrenalin everyone got performing was incredible. I was the official photographer and mom of the group. I made sure they went out when they needed to. I got everyone's drinks. I had found my spot and I liked it. The best part of the show became breakfast after. We all would sit down and just unwind and tell stories of the night. Most people try to pick the guys up to go home with them after the show but all the guys want to do is unwind, eat and go to sleep. There is no energy for anything else.

CHAPTER 11

When we got back from the show we picked up a new gig at Sidewinders. It was run by a man named Gus. He had been performing as a drag queen for over 20 years. To look at him you would never know he did drag. He is a very scruffy older gentleman with a scruffy beard and he comes across very masculine. He is a very nice guy but you know when he shakes your hand because of the firm grip he is very upfront and like Pop always said a handshake tells the character of a person. He did drag on Friday nights and wanted the Boyz to dance after the drag show. Sidewinder was a country themed bar that didn't play country music. It was just a long bar with 2 bars one on the front and one in the back just off of the dance floor. For the longest time I didn't know there was another room with pool tables. The new dancer was the Canadians cousin. He told us that he was almost 21 but really wanted to dance. He told us that he was turning 21 in a month. We told him we would bring him into the group but he was not allowed to drink. His first time dancing with us was at Chris's House. He went over well there but they loved him at the country bar so that is mainly where he danced. Later on we found out how old he really was 18. Yea he isn't dancing with us till he turns 21.

This was hard for Michael because he was trying to pull together the group and now he was down a dancer. Michael and Felipe was still having issues with Teddy...Teddy knew Michael had hooked up with Felipe the night they were all supposed to go out which I didn't but Teddy didn't know that Michael had asked me to hook up with him again...which for me was their first time.

So far this year had been filled with our 1st big show which Michael pulled off with by the skin of his teeth…nobody would have known it from what the people saw. It was such a good show they wanted us out again in November. I am so proud of all that he has done for himself and his family. I have never seen a man more dedicated to his family…he puts his heart in soul in all that he does…and I thank him for that. So coming to the end of the year the next opportunity for Michael was Halloween.

That Halloween Michael wanted to do the costume contest at Chris's because it gave him the opportunity to get him some exposure to increase his fan base and an opportunity to network for the Boyz. Figuring since he won the prior year at Tree Top he wanted to do it again. Which would be good for him, the group and it would bring money in for the family. He figured to kill 2 birds with one stone he would invite Felipe out to be able to spend some time with him since he really had not gotten any face time with him because usually when he saw him we were at the bar or there were other people around. I didn't mind because we had been have date nights which were amazing with lots of dancing and laughing together.

Michael had put together a play off the Jack of Hearts costume he won with last year. He continued with his erotic Wonderland and became a sexy white rabbit. He had bought white spandex chaps that had a bell bottom flare at the end of the legs. He wore this over a black thong with fur that barely covered his ass. The white suspenders continued the costume upwards towards the white studded leather choker. The costume was finished off by a black top hat he had attached white bunny ears with a white silk long scarf that hung down his back. The white gloves just pieced it all together. He looked amazing.

I told him to call me after the contest so I could hear how the night went. I kissed him as he left wearing the outfit which was hardly anything. The only thing that kept him covered was a shoulder to floor black cape. He looked really good but really cold. He took care of gas and cigs before he got in the costume although I know the ladies at the gas station would have loved to see him.

He met Felipe outside of Chris's. Felipe showed up in a pirate costume which Michael said was very sexy and that he looked very good in. Michael went over and got into Felipe's car when he got a phone call from his mom. She told him that the kids really didn't have anything to eat and she wanted him to go and buy them food. Michael was going to wait outside for Felipe to return but decided to go in and register for the contest, stay warm and get a drink while he waited on Felipe to get back.

When Felipe got back the two of them went out to the smoking area to talk and actually get to know each other. This though didn't go well. Michael is known at the bar and gets interrupted a lot when he is trying to talk to someone but this night it was some stupid female that liked to hear the sound of her own voice and didn't know how to act in a gay bar. She kept interrupting them saying that they were so good looking...they looked so good together...that they made such a cute couple...she had never seen two better looking men.

Here is a hint for all the females that come into a gay bar...just have a good time...gay men don't need to hear your thoughts on who they are with or how good they look and most don't want to hear from you anyway because you are invading their space. The gay bar is for those who want to escape the judgmental looks and bullshit they get from a lot of people in the straight world. This is a place where they go to be themselves. Straight couples are invading gay bars for whatever reason...there are many other bars for you to go to why don't you just go there. Gay people are not circus freaks...they do not need you gawking at them like a spectacle. If you come in to see a drag show...come on in...drink (not water and not one drink split between 3 of you) ...tip the drag queens and the bartenders...and stay in your seat. They do not need your help on stage. Being invited up is different but if they don't ask...stay in your seat. Be friendly but don't stand around talking so loud that you are making sure that everyone knows you are straight and that your husband is at home taking care of the kids. Just FYI...which I have heard a million times...if a gay bar is the only bar your husband/boyfriend is fine with you coming to by yourself...you need a new husband/boyfriend. If he doesn't trust you at straight clubs you have a problem. Every time I hear that all I can think is how pathetic you are and how sad your life must be. So...if you have to come into the gay clubs then don't make an ass of yourself by trying to be the center of attention...so...if you come in...just have a drink...enjoy the music...STAY QUIET AND STOP ACTING LIKE YOU ARE AT A STRAIGHT BAR...MEN ARE NOT GOING TO TREAT YOU SPECIAL THEY DON'T LIKE FEMALES THEY ARE INTO MEN. Anyway Michael and Felipe sick of her interrupting every 2 seconds decided to go inside and wait till the contest started.

Michael did the contest. Unfortunately he didn't even place because there were so many good well thought out costumes that night. Fuk U and Fuk Me from the movie Austin Powers won. After the contest was over they went back to the smoking area but this time they decided to sit in a darker area where they wouldn't be bothered by a lot of people. There were not a lot of people in this area which would give them to quieter more intimate atmosphere they were after.

Michael and Felipe sat very close to each other and started talking. Michael learned that Felipe had been a choreographer as well as a stripper while he was telling him about the Rumors show coming up. He offered to pay Felipe to help him come up with a group number for the next show. Felipe jumped at the chance to work with Michael but told him he didn't want any money. Michael told him he would have to pay him something. The two continued talking, laughing, having a good time getting to know each other.

Meanwhile I woke up about 12:30 in the morning and Michael had never called. I was getting worried because I had not heard from him since he left. I texted his phone several times and even called. I also texted Felipe's phone and got nothing. It was now past 1:30 and I had heard nothing. I know my internal fears stem from losing children but I can't help it. It scares me. He told me he would call and he had not yet. My mind went to wondering if they had even made it. I called Teddy and asked him to go and see if he was at Chris's. Teddy called me back and said Michaels car was there. I told him thanks for checking for me; sorry that I called and made him nervous too which made him drive down for me. I told him to have a good night and that I would talk to him later. Michael called not to long after that and told me he was ok which always calms me down when I hear his voice.

Now what I didn't know till Michael got home is what transpired in the bar. Michael was standing in front of Felipe and Felipe had his hands on his ass when Teddy walked up behind them. Teddy had angry black man face on when he spoke loudly and very clearly telling him that he needed to get home and call me so you need to get going. Now I would have loved to be a fly on the wall because knowing both the way I do the testosterone from both at that second would have filled the bar. Michael asked why he needed to get going and Teddy said because I said so. Michael being Michael told Teddy that I knew where he was so he didn't need to leave buy Teddy didn't care and told him to get going. Now people were watching and listening to what was going on and Michael didn't want it to come to blows or air any more dirty laundry told Teddy that his cape was upstairs to which Teddy told him to get it. Michael told Felipe bye…no hug…no nothing because when Michael turned around Teddy restated loudly…GET GOING. As Michael started to walk up the stairs Teddy told him he would wait outside for him but didn't leave until Michael made it up the stairs. When Michael made it outside Felipe was across the street so he tried to talk to Teddy but all Teddy would say is get home as he walked off. Michael headed across the street to his car parked beside Felipe's when he saw Teddy standing staring at him with angry black man face so as Michael past Felipe's car he said talk to you later.

When Michael got home I told him I wouldn't have sent Teddy to make sure he was ok if he had called me. I had nobody I could turn to but Teddy. I asked Michael why he didn't call and he told me that he had left his phone in the car. We had a conversation that night. I found out that he did think about calling me but because he had left the phone in the car he didn't want to walk back out to the car to get it. I know Teddy showing up made him wish he had taken the 5 minutes out of his night to walk right across the street and called me. That really bothered me. I didn't care that Teddy had caught Michael and Felipe together because it was all on Michael for not calling.

Michael didn't talk to Teddy very much after that well actually Teddy didn't answer Michael's text. Not that they talked a lot but Teddy was a bit upset and I don't blame him. Michael couldn't spend a lot of time on Teddy because he had a show to worry about. Felipe and Michael started texting and talking every day. Michael wanted a main dance number to open the show this time and he wanted Felipe to help. He talked to Mike, the gentlemen who manages Chris's, about practicing upstairs. He told Michael that he didn't care he set rehearsal up.

Chris's was the perfect place to rehearse because it had mirrors at either end of the dance floor so they could see what they were doing. I went to rehearsals when I could but it was mainly to see Rick and Fernando. I loved the dance. I couldn't go this time with Michael because of our youngest so Michael went by himself. Michael was going to meet everyone up there. Felipe was the first to arrive. Michael told Felipe that the boys were going to be late so they started practice without them.

During practice there was a bit of touching going on that would normally happen during practice but because of the way Michael ad Felipe were this caused sexual tension between them. To explain more Michael and Felipe tried to keep their distance from each other and keep this time professional and trying not to be to into each other. Neither one of them were touchy feely type of people so the sexual tension caused some issues for them to stay this way. It was new for both of them and they wanted to be with each other sexually. Every time they saw each other it was not convenient for them to really express physically what they wanted.

Michael decided to take himself out of the situation by going to the bathroom which was taking a bit longer since he was hard. Looking up he noticed in the mirror that Felipe was leaned back on the couch that was on the dance floor staring at his ass. A few minutes later Felipe disappeared out of his line of sight. Felipe appeared at the bathroom door. Michael just shook his head and smiles when he saw Felipe adjust himself. The next second Felipe was behind him and pulling his hips towards him. Now I am going to stop there for a few reasons 1... because I am not writing a Jackie Collins novel and 2... I don't want to hear the rest of the story because I am just finding out and I don't want to hear about his sexual escapades.

Two weeks later we were at Rumors again. Everyone their loved us. There were not as many people since we had just been there about 2 months ago but there was still a decent amount of eagerly awaiting fans to see some skin.

As you walk in you can see the whole bar except the dressing rooms where the entertainment would get ready. It was one of the largest we had ever been able to use it was very nice...now it was tucked away in the left back corner of the bar behind a make-shift curtain. There is a pool table as soon as you walked in the door and when you round the corner looking into the bar there were high and low tables for seating. The only bar in the place was off to the right. The bathrooms were down a hallway off to the right and a large mirror filled the wall at the end of the dance floor which was between the rows of seating on either side. The raised D.J. booth separated the bar and the row of seating on the right side of the dance floor.

Michael took Rick, Fernando, the Canadian and Baby Face with him for the show. Like I said every show has drama but this time it was mainly between Fernando, Baby Face and the Canadian. Now there are the usual groping but the love triangle going on between these three kept you head spinning. If the three weren't humping each other on the dance floor as part of a gogo set they were huddled in the back. Although I didn't go to the back much because I was busy on the floor but one of the times that I did I realized I had not seen the Canadian out front and he was not in the back. Just FYI when he drinks you really need to watch him. So I went searching. I finally found him outside in the front of the bar by the street talking to people in his underwear. Yes...you're right if you keeping track of the seasons it is winter.

Felipe showed up almost at the end of the show. I found this odd because he wasn't part of the show. I took him to the back to talk to Michael. It was at the half way point where we take a 15 minute break so that everyone can get a drink, pee, and smoke. When the show started again Felipe latched himself to me like bees on honey. People kept asking if he was going to strip because he is adorable. He would just smile and shake his head no. I tried to play it up by lifting his shirt but I noticed this made him very uncomfortable so I stopped.

You know I really enjoy the shows. They are extremely stressful because of all the things I do. I have to make sure all the guys are ok, get all their stuff including money and clothes picked up, talking to the DJ, making sure the right music is played for each dancer, dealing with the bar owner, getting the money, paying everyone, making sure the guys are where they need to be and on time, taking pictures and video and this is just to name a few. Yes it is stressful and when it is over or during the last number when all the guys go out and dance I get to go to the bar and get me a well-deserved coke. I wouldn't change a thing though.

Now the best part of the whole trip was between Felipe and Rick. That night Felipe had to sleep with Rick. Rick and I had Felipe convinced that Rick slept with a razor blade under his pillow. Felipe being as skittish as he was...the idea of Rick having a razor blade under his pillow made him very nervous. Not to mention Rick would say and do things towards him sexually just to see the reaction. It was a great evening. The razor blade, though, was the funniest.

Every movement that Rick made that night made Felipe jump. I have never laughed so hard because at one point Felipe jumped so hard he fell off the bed. This was not the only time he jumped off the bed but it got funnier and funnier the more times we could make him do it. The next morning Michael went over to him while he was sleeping and barely touched him and he shot out of bed onto the floor. It also helped because Felipe couldn't see very well. I love my boys they are amazing.

Speaking of the Boyz Felipe started dancing with us. Felipe had been dancing at Sidewinders and Chris's with us for a couple of months. Felipe is a 6'2: lighter skinned Latino and German man with black hair and dark eyes. He has very broad shoulders, a nice chest and great arms. He has the thickest eyelashes that make him look like he is wearing eyeliner but he isn't. Most women would kill for his lashes. One of my favorite things is his smile and laugh. He can light up a room with his smile.

Felipe started coming out when he wasn't dancing but Michael was dancing to hang out. When he would he never left my side except when I was taking pictures. We did a lot of talking so I got to know him. Yes...there were some things that still were off about him and Michael and I talked about that but I loved to hang out with him. I found out that he was highly ticklish just by touching his side while I talked to him and that made me happy because he would laugh and jump and I loved his smile and laugh.

One night Michael told us he had a new dancer showing up. I was sitting in the back where the guys got dressed talking to Felipe and helping him put on the concealer...they use to cover any blemishes. I always went to the back to talk to the guys. This is where I would get to know all the guys... that and shows... but we would sit back and just talk about everything. They also came to me when they needed anything. The conversations would go between stuff at the bar to family, friend, boyfriend, or work issues they were having. Sometimes the conversations would be so in-depth that Michael would come back and see where they were...anyway...back to that night. So Michael had told us that this guy was going to show up and while I was back talking to Felipe in walked this amazing looking man built like a shit brick house with a personality that consumed the room. Felipe and I instantly loved him. He stood back there talking to us for a long time before

Michael came back. As he walked in we introduced him to Prime. Come to find out this wonderful man had been seen doing karaoke by Bill, the D.J. at Chris's, and Bill told him he needed to talk to Michael and that he should dance for the Boyz. The night Prime had come to karaoke it was only the 2nd time he had been to a gay club because he had been in the military and after that his boyfriend he dated for a long time didn't like to go out. So he was new to the area and the gay club environment. I was thankful that Bill had sent Prime to us because I loved him from the start and that was only confirmed the more time I got to spend with him.

Now the dancer that Michael was talking about was Drake. Now when Drake showed up we all realized he was built like a shit brick house too and the same height as Prime about 5'8". Prime had sandy brown hair and beautiful eyes where Drake was dark haired and dark eyes. Drake's skin tone was more tan than Prime's. Drake had danced for Chippendale's and was currently working with 3 agencies who hired out strippers. Odd note though Drake was straight and had never done gogo let alone dance at a gay bar. He was friends with Fernando and found out about the group through him. He had gay friends and was comfortable around them which is why he was not bothered by dancing for the Boyz.

Felipe and I found him to be the exact opposite of Prime. Drake came across very cocky. This made me wonder if he was going to be a good fit for the group because everyone in the group acted more like family and Drake seemed to be more into himself.

Prime started dancing with the group. Now I use the term dancing loosely because well...ya...he was to that good. He loved it and put all he had into it but it needed work. The crowd loved him and his body was to die for and the pictures I too of him turned out so good. His interaction with the crowd and the other dancers came so natural. All of them dance together and on each other trying to give the crowd what they want...and trust me they want it. They do their best to entertain and give everyone a good show. On that note I do need to say something to all the men and women who love to watch them.

About tipping..this is how the Boyz make their money. So if you like what you see tip. That does not mean change...ARE YOU KIDDING ME!! YOU CHEAP BASTARDS!! If all you're going to do is dig in the bottom of your purse or pocket and dig out change don't bother coming up and taking a free feel. This has actually happened to one of our dancers. That story is for another time but this rant I will put in at this time. They all work very hard to look as good as they do. All dancers put on a show to entertain the crowd. They pay attention to the ones tipping.

You want attention tip them. Don't be afraid that is what they are there for. They are there for your entertainment. You come to the bars to see the dancers why stand in the back worried what people will think of you because they are there for the same reason. I have not once seen someone walk in just to drink and not watch the dancers. Something else while we are on the subject of tipping ... please do not think that your little dollar will get you there attention for the night. It's a dollar. Let me break this down for you so you will understand better.

They have to pay a gym membership where they devote a lot of their time and effort. Most spend 4 or 5 days a week for 2 or 3 hours a day working out. Their meals most of them are on are a strict dietary routine so they will look the way they do and we all know health food is not cheap. They also spend money on all the underwear they wear. Just so you know they are not getting them from Wally World. They spend $15 up to $100 sometimes on one pair of underwear to look good for you ...the crowd... the fans. The outfits they wear whether they are homemade or not cost money. To become someone's fantasy takes imagination on the dancer's part to put together a good costume from top to bottom. So let me break it down money wise for you. They spend about $750 - $950 a month just to look good for you. So if you think your little $1.00 will get you all the night attention you want I'm here to tell you.....You Are Wrong. So show that you enjoy them dancing and creating a stimulating atmosphere and tip them.

Most women dancer brings in $600 a night but in the gay world nobody tips very much. The women don't get groped on like the Boyz do and they make way more money. Sad that people who tip them feel that they should get stuff for free. Most of the time people who come to the gay bars think they should be able to get something for nothing and be able to grope and play for however long they want. Another point I have to mention is that during the shows women do come to see the Boyz and when they are the ones tipping then don't bitch. When the men don't show up or sit back and not walk up to them and tip then don't complain when the women are getting more attention.

So the next time you want to say ...oh anyone could do that...they are not that hot...they are just stuck on themselves...remember they work very hard to look like that and no not everyone could/should be able to. So an honest look in the mirror might be what you need to do. They use the tip money to pay their bills...buy more stuff to look good for you... SURVIVE...that is what they use the money for. Also if you think a dollar will get you all you want think again. The Boyz are here for the gay community. This is the first group, to my knowledge, that will let you touch them and interact with them. They are all gay or bi so they are here for this community. Show you care and appreciate what they are doing. I'm just saying because I wouldn't let you touch me for a dollar let alone try to stick it up my hole and then sneak a feel on your way out. They love to dance show them you appreciate what they are doing and honestly tip them. Anyway sorry about the rant but I really think everyone needed to hear that...so back to the story I was telling you about Prime and Drake.

Drake had a hard time too because stripping is different from gogo. Stripping is about a routine that you come up with set to music and the people are there to tip. Gogo is different because you are there subjected to whatever the D.J. plays and you are trying to entice people to come up and tip.

On a side note to all D.J.'s...you are there to entertain your audience if you have a younger crowd then you need to take that into consideration. Which means the music needs to be within their lifetime...something that they have heard. JR always said he played 4 or 5 hard hitting songs with a tribal beat that people knew and could really get into. Then he would play 2 or 3 good songs but maybe not as well-known because this gave people time to go to the bathroom and get a drink. Also, the busier the dance floor the more money the boys make...the more money the bar makes. Unfortunately when D.J.'s play what they want whether it is good or not or play a lot of tinkle sounds that last for a minute...1 it is hard to dance to without looking stupid and 2 it is the fastest wat to clean off the dance floor. Guess what this means...no money for the bar, bartenders, bar backs or the dancers. If you want to serve your own agenda and play what you want without considering what it is doing to the people who hired you then don't take the job...go home and listen to your IPod...you are there to do a job...DO IT!! Ok sorry another rant but that is just what I have seen and learned over all the time I have spent in the bars…so anyway.

Prime and Michael were dancing one night at Chris's when the D.J. from Fantasy came in and saw them. He really wanted them at the bar he worked for. After talking to Michael on Facebook they finally set a date. It took a bit longer than usually because every time they came up with a date the owner would come back and say that date was taken. After seeing Michael and Prime those were the two he wanted. He would have liked more but nothing happened and he didn't really put forth that much effort.

I didn't go on many of the gogo events because there is not to much for me to do except take pictures and that can get really boring since I don't know anyone. I guess I could always just stay on the floor and take pictures all night but I don't want to do that. So I have decided not to go but I still wanted pictures. Felipe was an amateur photographer so he went to take pictures. I felt a bit of satisfaction from this because he would tease me saying some of my pictures were blurry. I knew he would understand after he went and tried to take pictures just how I felt and that it was not easy.

The 3 set off on their trip. This was really the 1st time Michael, Felipe and Prime had got to spend any time together. Prime really liked Felipe…he thought he was a big loveable goof and he thought Michael was really cool. Felipe thought Prime was a nut but loved him all the same Michael loved Prime he thought he was a riot, quirky, funny and very different from the rest of the guy because of his loud and boisterous personality.

Michael and the guys had to wait for a while for the D.J. to come get them so he could show them around the bar and where they could get ready. The guy checking the id's told the Boyz that the place needed new blood and it was about time they got some fresh, well-built nice looking professional men to come in and show there dancers what they were missing. Everyone walking through the door agreed.

The night had only 2 problems. The first problem was the other so called dancers. The main problem with the other dancers except one who had a good personality named Superman. The problem with the dancers were their over inflated ego's…one of the dancers were the worse. He had crowned himself "King of the Dancers". He was not that attractive in any way shape or form. This dancer tried to show up Prime that night but Prime just thought he was a snobby twinky guy and didn't have to do anything he let his body talk for itself. The one decent guy out of the whole group talked to Prime most of the night. The 2nd issue was the music. The bar played hip hop and top 40 music most of the night until it turned midnight then it went all hip hop. Unfortunately this made the bar turn all hood and the money stopped. That pretty much ended the night.

When the guys got back after the gig Felipe apologized saying he couldn't get a good picture either. That it was hard to take pictures of moving people in a dark room with lights changing in a blink of an eye. On a side note it is good that someone else sees my pain.

One of the things Michael and I talked about was Felipe. I told Michael that I didn't want them sleeping in the same bed because I was the only one he should sleep with, cuddle with and wake up to. I figured out of everything I let Michael do this was the least he could do for me. He told me that they didn't sleep in the same bed together...and I have no proof to the contrary so I have to believe him. Ya...I know what you're thinking...me too but without any proof I have to go on his word.

Felipe and Michael began talking and texting a lot. It didn't really bother me because I knew he was just a toy. Michael can separate the two... sex and friendship. Even though the holidays are for family and friends Felipe had become a friend not just a toy. So...I said ok...when Michael asked if Felipe could come over for Christmas that year. Felipe had issues with his family and I didn't want him to feel out in the cold so he came over for dinner. Besides that year had changed anyway Fernando had gotten him and Michael a gig for New Year's Eve which I didn't mind since we really needed the money. The year was ending and we had made it through another one.

CHAPTER 12

Things for the group were going along fine and so were Michael and I … until the day we got a phone call. Michael had picked me up that day from work to sneak away for breakfast. We did this as often as we could to have adult alone time away from everyone else. The look on his face as he was talking to the person on the phone was not good. After he hung up the phone he told me that someone had named him as one of their partners and that he needed to be tested for Gonorrhea. We found it odd because there was no signs at all or never had been. I didn't know a lot about it but Michael did because of his days when he ran a group home.

Michael drove up to have blood work done. They told him that it would be back in about a week. So now we were playing the waiting game. They didn't tell us who reported him as a partner or wouldn't give us any information. I will never understand this because I feel the person who is being tested should know who gave them what. I don't agree with someone just telling you someone might have made you sick and you need to come in and be tested.

Requesting a day off for Michael's job took a bit of time. I had lost my job during this period so I was at home when a gentleman came to the door. When I answered the door the man asked if Michael was home because he needed to talk to him. When I told him no he handed me an envelope and said it was confidential and I was not to open it just give it to Michael.

On a side note when a man comes to the door telling the person, who is the wife of the person they are asking to talk to, and tells them it is a confidential matter and not to open the envelope…what do you think they are going to do. Really anyone would open the envelope that said health department. I cannot believe someone would actually think the person who is opening the door…wife or girlfriend…not to open the letter. You know they are because you are talking about the health of the one they live with and love.

Now the other thing is they came to your house to drop off a letter that means it is serious. If I had not already known what was going on I would have been scared to death. When does the health department come to your house and tell you they have a serious health matter to discuss with you. For the one person the letter is for this is B.S. because it is their personal business. The letter should have never been left and they should not announce who they are or why they want to talk to them. For the ones who are in the dark it is a good way for the recipient to keep themselves healthy especially because men lie.

I know that many men lie about their extracurricular activities. Especially when it comes to this subject because of the fallout from people finding out their secret and how they are treated by the people finding out. I know one guy who steps out on his wife all the time. He doesn't care whether or not he uses protection and then sleeps with his wife unprotected. I know this because I heard she just had a baby. He sleeps around with anyone and can because of his job. His hours allow him to come and go whenever he wants so she would never know. If I ever meet her I will tell her because of what her husband has done. So for someone like her yes the letter should be delivered and handed to her so she can keep herself and her kids safe.

Honesty in a relationship is crucial. When you don't have honesty you cannot have a healthy relationship. I know my husband has lied to me over many things and has caused our marriage many problems. I do not trust everything he says and because of this it does causes problems. You cannot have a healthy relationship like this. We have worked through all the lies but I still, being honest with myself and you, I still don't trust everything he says. When you way the pro's and con's I understand why he lied about it all so that is why I stay. I am very realistic. I know that the lies he has told have not been life altering ones. Some of them could have been but were not so for me I choose to move on with my life.

All I can do is hope that the lies he tells now will not hurt our marriage. Michaels' marriage is very important to him and always has been. There are just lapse in judgment on his part to his warped sense of being. In short sometimes he doesn't think things through completely he just acts. Looking though in a very rational way without any emotion I know beyond a shadow of a doubt that Michael and I will be together forever because if there was a raft and only 5 could be on it...hands down I know it would be me and the kids and the grandbaby. I know that you might think this is being a hypocrite or wishy washy but part of it comes from my emotion and the sound part comes from logic and rational thinking. So the gentleman coming to the door I have a problem with but because of this it keeps people honest in their behavior.

Waiting for the day we could find out was unbearable. We had to wait almost two weeks because of Michael's job. He worked during their business hours so he had to ask off for a day to go. I was ready to go anytime. We talked about all of them and we told each other that no matter what we found out we would make it through it.

I did a lot of praying that once they confirmed what it was they would cure him and all would be fine. We had stopped having sex since we got the phone call a few weeks ago. He did not want to take the chance of making me sick with whatever we were dealing with. Until we knew for sure what we were dealing with he was not going to take the chance to pass it along. We didn't need to use protection because I couldn't get pregnant anymore and he was using protection when he was with everyone else. Well so we thought.

We made an appointment to go and find out the results. They took Michael to the back and left me sitting out in the waiting room. I couldn't focus on anything I had so many things running through my head that it was like I had nothing there. I was scared for him and I was scared for me and my children because of how Michael would take the news if it was bad. Time seemed to drag on forever. I am glad that I was the only one in the waiting room because I began to break down several times before pulling it together. I was out there what seemed to be forever when I decided to go outside to smoke a cigarette. I stood by the door so that I could see if anyone came out to the room. When I saw the gentleman walk down the hall my heart stopped so I rushed back inside and just looked at the door wondering if I should go in and see if he was ok. All I wanted to do was hold him and let him know how much I cared. Tears filled my eyes that I wiped away and reach for the door. Just then Michael came out of the bathroom. His eyes were red and I could tell he had been crying…he told me later that he had gone into the bathroom and broke down. I knew instantly by the look on his face what the news was.

My heart instantly broke for him and all I could do was hug him. There were no words spoken except I love you and we will make it. He grabbed hold of me and just hugged me tightly and I him. Michael put his head on my shoulder and we just stood there forever holding each other.

When Michael walked back into the room and I broke down crying. I had only cried one other time like that and that is when our twins died. I sat there trying to stop because I knew they would be coming out for me but I couldn't. The life changes this meant for us and our family although at this point we didn't know anything. Finally I pulled myself together and a second later they came out Michael came out and asked me to come back.

The man sitting back there asked Michael if it was ok for him to talk to me about what they had been talking about. Michael told him yes she knows everything. The gentleman told me that Michael had HIV and what he knew about the illness. I already knew that since I saw Michael in the hallway. The first thing he told me was that his partner has been positive for many years and he was still negative so there was no reason Michael and I couldn't have a healthy sex life. That was the furthest thing from my mind at the time. I was worried about Michael he looked lost and broken. I had never seen him like this before and I was scared. When we lost the kids he looked lost but this was different.

A lady came into the room and asked if it was ok to take me back into another room and administer the test on me. I hated leaving Michael I knew he needed me but I also knew that finding out if I was sick would help him. As the lady and I walked back she began to ask me if I knew how Michael had contracted the disease. I said yes and she began to tell me, in a subtle way without coming right out and saying anything, that I didn't have to put up with it and I could leave especially if I was negative. This really dumbfounded me. I'm sure the look on my face was WTF…but I just wanted to get back to him and I didn't need to get kicked out because I kicked her ass.

She took me into a room and explained what she was about to do and then she administered the test. She continued to babble about whatever I don't really remember all I wanted was the results so that I could get back to Michael. I cannot imagine what Michael was going through. I needed to be with him.

I was negative and the first thing I could think of was to tell Michael so he would not be worried. She wanted to talk more to me but I stood up and told her I needed to get back to my husband but thanks for the advice I wouldn't need it. I found it in bad taste for her to say these things to me but my mind was focused on Michael or I would have told her just that.

As I walked through the door Michael turned around and looked at me. He looked so lost and empty. With a slight smile on my face...hoping it made him smile...I said I'm fine and he got tears in his eyes. You could see relief sweep over his face. With tears in my eyes I walked over and hugged him. I wanted to break down and let him know we would be fine but we are not alone so I didn't. The gentleman continued to talk about what it meant to be sick and what the illness was and how it worked. All of this I didn't know. I knew nothing about the illness. It is sad to say that I really thought that anyone who had it were dirty sex fiends who went around having unprotected sex with anyone. I remember Michael looking on line for guys to hook up with and if it said they were positive it was a total turn off and it was for Michael too. Who would want to sleep with a person like that? My mind had changed since then and I see things a bit more clearly now.

The man continued to talk to us was very nice. He told us that his partner had been positive for pretty much their whole relationship and he had remained negative. He told us that he and his partner had even had unprotected sex a few times over their relationship on special occasions and he was still negative. Not that he recommended that but he knew we were married and that might be a concern.

He told us lots of information that day. Oddly enough bottoms are more prone to get the illness. The micro tears that happens when something is inserted into a man makes them more susceptible to the disease. He went on to say that it is a lazy disease and unless it bumped into a CD4 protein cell in your body that is just floats around and dies. The micro tears open up the skin and allows them to get into the blood stream.

The last thing that he told us was that we would survive together. A good support network was important and not to tell anyone you did not trust or feel comfortable with. HIV was not life threatening anymore. He compared it to Diabetes. Although the stigmatism that goes along with it is still out there so unless you trust someone do not tell them. As long as you take your meds on time then the disease could be managed. The medication could make you undetectable. That doesn't mean you are not sick anymore but your viral load is so low that it doesn't show up in your blood work. He said the lymph nodes are where the virus has been found. There have been studies done where they took couples where one person had the illness and the other did not. When they finished the study nobody had contracted the disease from their undetectable partner even though they were having unprotected sex. Well the ones who stayed monogamous. They knew they had stepped out because the strain they had was different than their partners. He went through a lot of information that day but what he didn't explain to us was the emotional roller coaster someone goes through when they find out they are sick.

Michael and I talked about some things on the way home but not much. He was still processing the news. He was very thankful I was not sick and he said that to me many times. Now it was time to tell Teddy and Felipe. They both knew about the phone call with the mysterious illness. They both knew he was going in today to get the results. Michael wanted to make sure they were not sick too.

Michael told Felipe in the car, because he had called me a few times while I was waiting. Felipe is a nice guy…he really is. When he called he would ask if I was ok and wanted to know if Michael had found out anything yet. Michael told him where to go so he could be tested. Michael knew I was ok and he wanted to make sure everyone he had been with was safe. When we got home he talked to Teddy and told him to go get tested and he told Michael he was going to the doctor and would be tested then. Then he called his client the only one he had been with in a long time only to find out he had it too. Michael had not been doing clients because we had been so busy with the group and life.

Felipe called a bit later and wanted to come down for a minute. Now I am going to take a minute to say to everyone in the health care field…You are in a field where people are coming to you because they are worried, in pain, or have something that is bothering them they need to find out about. The way Felipe was treated when he went in to get tested was appalling. First he had some woman who just looked at him and asked in a rude way…what did he want and when he told her the behavior got worse. She asked, in a very disgusted way, if he was having sex with men and when he said yes she just rolled her eyes and told him to wait. Now let me explain something if that had been Michael her head would have been off her shoulders because they are already nervous coming in and taking the test...and you are going to make them feel like they are bothering you and that they are not worth talking to...I would have bitch slapped her. I do not give a flying fuck who you think you are...you don't give someone dirty looks or roll your eyes or be short with someone just because they say yes I have slept with a man. They are scared enough worrying about themselves where does this person get off treating him this way. I wish we would have gone with him because she would have felt like dirt the way he made Felipe feel. So all of you in that field remember if it wasn't for "sick" people you wouldn't have a job. So pay attention when they teach bed-side manner in med school and if you don't like your job get another one and save us all from looking at you. Felipe was not infected so that made us happy. For me and Michael though...the emotions were just beginning.

I was sad, mad, frustrated, worried, anxious, and actually I couldn't tell you what I was because there were so many things running through my mind at the time. I wanted him to be ok. I didn't want him to be sick. I didn't want to watch him fall ill and die. This is my soul mate. He is my everything and now he was carrying a death sentence around with him. How would this affect us? How would this affect our family? How would this affect him? How would this affect our sex life? Would he ever feel safe to be with me again? I had so many thoughts none of which I could share with him right now. He was my best friend I had no one to talk to except him. I needed him to tell me everything was going to be ok but he was the one in need. It was a very long and sad, confusing day all the way around. The gay side had taken my husband from me. They had already interfered with my life so much and now this. Once again I hated all things gay. Michael was headed down a dark path and I was not sure where we would end up. I was scared.

I feel that I need to take a few moments to say something to someone who I hope is reading this book not just for me but for all the people you have screwed over. I should also add this note for the ones that this behavior talks about. Michael always made sure he wore protection and the one he was with wore protection. I guess at least one time the person topping lied. I want to put in here a note to those types of people. You are scum of the earth. You have no regard for anyone but yourself and should be shot.

You didn't consider Michael, me, his kids, or his grandbaby all you thought about was gratifying your own selfish needs. Whether or not you knew you had something and that you could pass something on to someone else or not you were supposed to wear protection and I know Michael made sure. You will reap what you sow and I hope it is not good for you. I hope that your life is nothing but a mess...I hope that everyone you care about leaves because you are not worth loving. I know that God is the only one that will pass judgment on you but I know that one day He will and I take pleasure in that. I understand that may not be a very Christianly attitude and I am sorry for that but like I always say...everyone's walk is their own... and I will have to deal with the repercussions of what I say and how I feel for myself just as you will have to worry about the countless lives you have ruined by your own selfish needs and desires.

Anyway the day we found out Michael was sick...as usual...life didn't stop...he had to dance that night for the group of people who made him sick. He was very quiet while he was getting ready. He didn't want to go and dance. He didn't want to dance for "these" people...he didn't want to fake it and be nice to "them"...he didn't want to even look at "them". He knew though that he had made a commitment and he had to go through with it.

We showed up just before he had to go on. We walked in as usual but it didn't feel usual to me. I felt that everyone could see the worry on my face and the sadness. I knew that everyone would bombard Michael and I was worried he would go off...but he played like nothing happened. I was so sad for him because I could see it in his eyes the destruction he wanted to do to the bar and the people in it. As we were standing at the end of the bar by the railing I look towards the door and in walked Felipe. This was the first time I had a genuine smile on my face. I looked at Michael and pointed and he smiled too. Felipe walked right up to Michael and gave him a very compassionate hug. I rubbed on Michael's back when Felipe grabbed hold of me too. At that moment in time all was right with the world. The three of us embraced each other and just stood there what felt like forever. As we all pulled away Michael told Felipe that it was good to see him. Felipe sat with me the rest of the night and that is where Michael came to as soon as he left the floor. Michael made it through the night but it didn't change the feelings he was having towards the gay community.

The next night was no different because he had to dance at Chris's. Felipe and I sat back in the corner talking all night. I could see Michael recoil from everyone who walked up to him...they couldn't but I did. The hatred and disgust in his eyes for himself and the community was still there. I mentioned to Felipe that if I wasn't around that Michael needed to be watched...Michael had thought about suicide one other time since I had known him and I left our daughter with him to show him he had something to live for...I didn't explain all of this to Felipe but I let him know that there was an issue and that he needed to watch him. I also told Felipe that Michael was worried that he was going to leave now because he was sick. Felipe looked at me and told me that he would keep an eye on him because he wasn't going anywhere. Felipe just let me talk and cry a bit on his shoulder that night which I will always thank him for. That night let me know what kind of person he was and made me feel even closer to him.

Michael would come over to us when he would get off the box and just stand there with very little emotion on his face. His fake smile was not fooling me I could see right through it. I went up to get Michael and I a drink and Felipe walked to the back where the boys got dressed to talk to Michael and tell him he wasn't going anywhere. The walked back out and Felipe gave him a hug and Michael started to break down and because people were watching he pulled away from Felipe and composed himself because he had to dance. I knew then Felipe was going to stay...I was very thankful for this.

We set up an appointment at the clinic they told us about. Michael and I are very private people and don't like talking to other people about ourselves. Imagine me trying to wright this book it was, at first, more like bullet points. Michael didn't like discussing this issue with 20 people. Every time he turned around they were asking him very personal questions. I think they should make a questionnaire that people can fill out so they don't have to keep telling the same story over and over. I felt horrible for my husband every time he had to tell the story.

After sitting with a counselor for about a half an hour they took him back to draw blood. When Michael came out he made the comment that vampires worked here and he wondered if he had any blood left. I just smiled because that was the first attempt at a joke he had made. They gave us some pamphlets and a book for him to read. I knew he wouldn't read them. Since all I knew was what the man had told me but I still had no idea about what emotions were about to come my way I looked forward to reading the book. I knew Michael had a bit more information because it was him stepping out and I know that he had read about it. Most of the stories you hear are not true. For instance I figured drinking after someone you could be infected but that is wrong. Also, and this I found odd you cannot get it if someone who has it gives you a blow job. Only a few cases that I read about, when it comes to oral, mainly dealt with rimming. I am not an expert but I have learned about it now. The information in the pamphlets was minimal and the book was a total waste of time.

I found no useful information in the book at all. Yes, it told me about the illness but the guy at the clinic had already done that. Actually he was very nice and answered all our questions. Well, mine, Michael did not really ask much. The book was this upbeat story about how it all worked out for this gay guy. How in the hell would that help us? There were so many unanswered questions like … What type of emotions was the person who was sick going to have? How do you help your spouse in all that they are going through? I am not gay or bi so how are we supposed to deal with this? How is a married bi man supposed to deal with this? How does a bi man tell his family? The book was all about being gay but they left out an important person … my husband.

All the questions about the illness were answered but the unanswered questions about all the emotions is what we needed. Even the counseling sessions were geared towards gay people. How can my husband and I survive this? We have all the love in the world for each other but would love be enough to overcome this? The guilt my husband was feeling; to think that the woman he loved…the mother or his kids…the person he wanted to grow old with…he almost gave her an incurable disease. They have books on grief for everyone but not on the emotions that come with someone like my husband. Why wouldn't they have something like this? This illness affects more than just gay people.

I cannot imagine what my husband was going through. The hurt, the depression, the sadness, the despair, and the anger he was filled with was changing him and I did not know how to help him. I was watching the man

I loved slip away and something dark and scary replace him. Once again we were faced with a path that we had to figure out on our own. First we had to work through an unconventional marriage that nobody understood let alone us and now this. This is uncharted territory that nobody talks about and here we are right in the middle of it.

He knew I loved him and was staying but the guilt for all he had done to me and now this was weighing down on him. He was glad I was staying; I staying this long always shocked him. I explained to him that we would make it through this trial too but he felt like he did not deserve it. All he wanted to do was crawl in a hole so nobody could bother him, be around him, talk to him, or count on him for anything. He wanted to be left alone he did not want anyone to need him because he did not deserve it; he was diseased.

It is very hard to watch someone you love feel this way, to never smile about anything. We had just welcomed our 1st grandbaby into the world a few months before and she could barely make him smile. I cried a lot when he wasn't around and sometimes I couldn't help it when he was. I knew this would probably end us. He was so distant. All of this was the first few weeks. I wondered how long all this would keep up. How long could he deal with this? Was there a light at the end of the tunnel?

We had a show coming up at Rumors again so Michael started having practice again to prepare for the show. Felipe came down to get Michael for practice. Felipe and Michael had come up with a group number at the beginning of the show again. After practice was over Michael told Felipe how he was feeling. He told Felipe that he was not mad at him for leaving because he knew he would. He understood why Felipe never would be with him again and that he didn't blame him for that either. Michael stayed away from people with HIV so he understood Felipe especially because he was such a germaphobe. Michael just wanted Felipe to understand that he did not blame him for leaving even though he did not want to lose him but that it was ok.

I was not there so I do not know how the whole conversation really went or the emotions that went on during the conversation. I only know what Michael told me. His face was different. The admiration Michael spoke about Felipe that night was all over his face. Michael told me that he had talked to Felipe and explained everything to him and that after the conversation Felipe told him that he was not going anywhere.

This meant a lot to Michael on many levels. He would not lose the guy who was becoming his best friend. Here was this guy who he had almost given a death sentenced too and he was going to stick around. Felipe was easy to talk to about things I didn't fully understand because I don't fully get the bi side of things and Felipe did. Felipe was new to this, according to Felipe, because he had only been with 2 other men and was not very comfortable with his bi side. Michael did not have to admit to anyone new that he was sick because he still had his buddy. All these things made Michael very happy and a bit confused he was not completely sure why Felipe was staying.

I know that meant a lot to him that Felipe did not make him feel like a leper. He felt like that all on his own. Michael told me that he really wanted both of us around. The way he explained it was with both of us there he felt complete and protected. I was his wife and mother of his kids who had been through so much with him and that he couldn't live without. Felipe was a guy who had not been around that much and with all his hang ups wanted to stay and because Felipe understood the bi thing. I knew that the best thing for Michael right now was for the both of to be around him. That is why I invited Felipe down to the house to hang out as much as I could. Michael would never ask because after everything I had put up with he wasn't going to ask his wife if his "friend" could come down and hang out.

Felipe started coming down to the house whenever he could. Actually, he started spending a lot of time at the house. Michael would sit right between us. He would touch both of us. When we were around he didn't look so lost. One of us was always with Michael. I was scared to leave him alone. This meant I wanted Felipe or I with Michael at all times. I knew this was best for Michael because of the way he was feeling. Michael felt like we were his security blanket and I was ok with giving him that. We were his protectors. We could save him from the world.

If this is how everyone feels when they find out I hope that the ones they tell understand the turmoil they go through. Give them the time they need to work things out for themselves. Be there when they need you to be but give them the space to heal. Believe in them and if they are not the high hopes kind of people don't always say things will get better. Let them feel bad sometimes and just listen. Everyone reacts different to hearing the news but you should know your friend or loved one so let them experience this in the way they need to. Do not push your feelings on them right now they are dealing with enough. Just be there for them.

Maybe it was different in our case because I wasn't bi and didn't fully understand that side and Michael is not gay so the feelings are different. I know being married the way we were and the love we have for each other might have made a difference. To anyone reading this please understand that no matter what they say they are scared. They now will always be looked at as unclean. They will have to admit to the world that they have a highly contagious disease that without medication for the rest of their lives they will be sick. So cut them some slack not everyone who is sick asked for it. Remember for these people someone didn't give a shit about them and forced them to take something that they now have to live with.

For those of you finding out it will get better. I know some of you will roll your eyes but it will. This is where you find out who your real friends are. This could be where you think about your life and how things need to change. Above all else though if you didn't want this to happen it is not your fault. You didn't ask for someone to force this on you. Yes you put yourself in the situation but they lied and they took advantage of you. HIV is manageable now so in time you will feel better about yourself. There will be days but that is to be expected.

CHAPTER 13

Now that the Boyz were taking off and getting a fan base and it was growing every day. We also picked up a new dancer...well not new...because he was the one nice guy we met at Fantasy...Superman. He was coming in to dance at Chris's a few times. He was a husky muscular guy with sandy blonde hair. He was quiet in his demeanor. He told Michael that since they were at Fantasy the other dancers really didn't talk to him and they were not having him dance much. Michael welcomed him into the group because he fit into the Bear community and a lot of people liked him.

So with another dancer the group was getting big so I created a Facebook like page for the Boyz for Michael to communicate with the fans and keep them interested. Michael had told all the Boyz to create a separate fan page with their stage name for all the fans to join. Creating this page pulled them away from their family page but still let them have access to them. The Boyz found that they had a fan base and followers too. I created a website too for the group. It wasn't much but you work with what you have. It looked good but it was not a professional website with flash videos and clips. Michael liked it so that is all that matters.

The Boyz were now dancing every Friday night at Sidewinders now. Tipsy, remember back on my first outing with my husband where I was pulled up on stage, this was the only drag queen I had actually ever seen perform...well and the ones that performed with her. On the first night I was there early and had sat down by the stage. The drag show started so I started watching the show. This lovely woman Opal made her way to the stage. She was not an over the tops scary drag queen she looked just like any normal performer. She was wearing a classy long dress and a great wig. I wish my hair would stay that curly.

She came out and moved around the stage singing and collecting tips. It was like she was actually singing the song. She didn't just stand still she moved around and danced. About half way through the song she began to approach me. Flash backs from Tipsy flooded my mind and I became uneasy. Opal took a hold of my hand still acting like she was singing and said, "I'm going to stand here with you because I cannot remember the words to the fucking song." From that point on I loved her. She is actually the first and only drag queen that I have ever tipped. As time goes on she and I have been able to spend time together and she is one of my best friends. She may not be in the book to much because most of our time is spent talking and having drinks outside of this realm.

Although, I remember one of the first nights we actually had time to sit and get to know each other. I had went with Michael to Sidewinders and found out she was not working. I sat with her all night and drank while Michael danced. I call her a her because that is how I met him. I actually didn't know the protocol on what I should say or what I should call her/him. At the time Tim, who was Opal, said when I am in drag I am Opal and when I am not I am Tim but so I do not confuse everyone reading I will just refer to him as Opal so that you don't get confused. Yes, I have confused people because I will flop back and forth in one sentence sometimes between his stage name and his real name. So to save us both time I will just say Opal.

So Opal and I sat most of the night and talked. I find it odd because she is like me. Her outlook on relationships and how she sees things are just the way I see them. I feel bad because I thought she would be different because she was gay. I would have thought things would have been different. They were not though she was just like me. She had the same issues in her relationship that I do. I began to see that the two worlds were not really different. They were just people like you and me with the same thoughts and feelings. I felt so bad because I had thought the worlds would have made us different but actually we were the same.

I began to wonder why the world hated them so much. I had been included into a world where I did not fit in because I was not like them but at the same time we were so much alike. I had witnessed all the anger towards them and really didn't understand it. These were my friends and even though I was different I wasn't. I had been so closed off and judgmental like the rest of the world. I felt horribly bad and was so glad my eyes were now wide open. I never even saw it coming but I had a whole new bunch of friends that I loved. Opal included me in her conversations and introduced me as me not Michael's wife which made me feel good. Throughout the night she included me in all her conversations without missing a beat.

I was happy to hear that Michael was bringing Opal to the show to sing and be the MC. This time we went to Rumors we took Prime, Felipe, Drake, Fernando, Superman and Opal. Now Opal rode with his boyfriend, Andy, and their friend Cassy. This sucked because I really wanted to spend time with her. Felipe and Michael came up with a kick ass routine for the opening number. This time nobody else was in it because nobody could come to practice. They looked great doing it. I took video of it and for the camera that I had it looked good. Prime and Opal did a really hot number that night to the old song "I Touch Myself" by the Divinyls.

Now this show was a bit more fucked up than the rest. Let me start by saying that at the end of the opening number Michael went down to do a move and split his pants completely open right down the seam...from the butt (total blow out) all the way down the leg. There was no fixing them they were toast. You can even see when it happens in the video. I don't use that part...lol. Also, since I had Andy and Cassy there I put them to work. Prime let me use his very nice and very professional camera to do all the videos. I gave Andy my camera and now I wish I hadn't or I would have given him better guidelines to follow because he seemed obsessed with this twinky bar-back. There was a shit ton of pictures of him when I downloaded all the pics...him walking, him standing, him bent over serving drinks, him smiling, him talking...get the point.

The rest of the mess came from backstage. Drake was taking GHB and pretty much overdosed himself so that he fell down the steps in the back by the dressing room that lead outside and made a scene outside by yelling and screaming that...he hurt...and arguing with people trying to help him get in the car. Michael finally...after Drake took a swing at Michael...picked Drake up and put him in Fernando's car. Now the story we heard later from Fernando was that Fernando and Drake did something while they were in the car before Drake past out...The World May Never Know.

Prime was also drugged that night. He didn't take any GHB from Drake but one of the customers must have slipped him something. I know this because as you know one of my many jobs is to make sure that I keep track of all the dancers. Well...when I went looking for Prime some guy had him by the arm and was walking him towards the door. When I walked up to him and asked what was going on the guy said that Prime was going home with him. Yes...the mom came out in me and I said no he wasn't...to which the guy said yes he was and I turned into bitch mom and took Prime nicely by the arm and looked at the guy and told him to get lost and told Prime that we were ready to leave. Prime told the guy bye and walked back talking to me as we walked. He went to breakfast with us and acted like nothing was wrong...except he kept his sunglasses on and sang the song "I Wear My Sunglasses At Night" by Cory Hart. We all thought he was just being goofy.

The next morning though we realized that this was not an act. It took us forever to wake him up and when we did he went into the bathroom and got sick. Walking back into the room babbling something he slumped over at the end of the bed in a praying position and past back out. It took us forever to wake him up. We were all very scared. Prime never acted like that ever even if he had been drinking the night before. Cassy drove his car home for him because he was in no shape to be driving.

Drake showed up the next morning very early knocking on the door before anyone was up. I walked to the door and opened it. When I saw Drake he asked for his money. I told him we had it but that he owed Fernando money for babysitting that night. Drake laughed it off and I told him I was serious because of the way he acted and because he did it to himself I would have left him there. I handed them their money and they left.

When we got back a guy who had danced with Michael when Scott was running things...remember he was the client that got Michael started dancing and just dropped off the face of the earth...well Hunter talked to Michael about dancing again. Scott had stopped using him because of something that happened to Hunter when he was younger and that he was over exposed because everyone knew him.

Hunter was this young looking Asian mix firecracker. He had a large personality with a heart of gold. He was very smart and very artistic. When he walked into the room you knew it. He would put together outfits like Michael would. When I first met him I thought he was to young to get into the bar. He was short and slender with black hair and dark eyes. His boyfriend Alex usually always came out with him. They were always together…when you saw one of them…the other was not far behind. I never really talked to Alex very much but he is a very sweet person…someone who can make you smile.

I should take a moment and tell ya that Michael has a good group of guys. The group had something for everyone. A wide range of body types and personalities and look wise there was something for everyone. Each guy had their own fans. Michael began getting messages on his Facebook asking him who was dancing. He has found over time though unless their favorite guy was dancing they wouldn't come out. So he has just started advertising that they will be there.

Speaking of Facebook I would like to take this opportunity to voice my opinion. I know that Facebook has a lot to deal with and most of it is not good. I think they should focus more on the illegal activities they run across and leave people alone. My husband has been ban from Facebook so many times I have lost count. All the people that are on his Facebook know what he does and everyone likes the pictures that he posts. If you are on his Facebook and do not like what you see…UNFRIEND HIM…don't report him so that he gets banned. Many other people like what he posts and do not have a problem. Facebook does that enough on their own which I find funny because there are woman showing their boobs and crotch all the time but they do not get banned. To me this looks like he is getting picked on. Just like Facebook told all drag queens they could not have a page with their drag queen name on it only their real name. To me that sounds like they are against gay people. I am sure Cher didn't have to get rid of her fan page. Opal had to so that just makes me wonder why Facebook has it in for gay people. That is just my opinion not trying to ruffle any feathers and I do not know that for sure. I am just saying it sounds like it to me. There are other photographers who have taken nude…but tasteful…pictures of men that Facebook has banned. Not to mention the porn stars Michael knows who have been ban for posting a fully clothed picture of themselves kissing their boyfriend. Anyway…back off my soap box.

We all spend time with each other when we are at the club talking and laughing. I have went to a birthday with Fernando and had a great time… Hunter, his boyfriend and I have talked many times at the club, Rick is such an open book that it is so easy to get to know him, Baby Face...the Canadians cousin...was just a very happy person and was a joy to talk to...the Canadian was so smart he usually lost me in the conversations when he started talking about his passion, Architecture...Felipe...well... he is so compassionate and caring that this makes him a wonderful man... Prime, well, all I can do is smile...he is just an amazing, playful, honest, opinionated, loving man...Drake, well, he is different, a good heart but he just comes across wrong to those who don't understand him.

Michael would switch up all the dancers each weekend. So depending on who was dancing where caused me to have more of a connection with some. I always went with Michael so the one dancing with him was the ones I got to know better. I will say though most of them have met the kids and our youngest has a crush on Prime but Rick was her first love...lol. Anyway where was I...so when we got back from the show Felipe started coming down to the house almost every weekend and some days during the week.

CHAPTER 14

At this time Felipe was spending even more time at the house. For me Michael and Felipe we would watch movies together...even though most of the movies Michael and I like Felipe didn't. Some of the movies we like we had to explain to him. This made things funny because he would hide behind a pillow when scary or bloody parts of a movie would come on. Actually the scary parts were not really scary but to him they were. Felipe had become part of the family, not just a toy or a dancer.

The three of us usually were at the house or at the club with one or both of them dancing so I decided we should all go out. Michael and I had not had a date night since he had been diagnosed so I invited Felipe with us too. We all had fun dancing with each other. I even told Michael to dance with just Felipe. The night was great.

One night when Michael was dancing at Chris's Felipe and I were sitting at the bar Blake worked. I and Blake were drinking as we usually did every time I went to the bar. So...when I drink I get very loving and a bit of a mess. Now don't get me wrong I can drink and I can hold my liquor but I get very happy and loving when I drink. So it was about 12:30 or 1 in the morning when Michael walked up to us and I wanted a kiss and he gave me one. After I got a kiss I told him to kiss Felipe and then me and then Felipe and then me...ya you can see how it went. I was having a good time. Blake would just laugh at me when I turned into a girl. Well, tonight, Michael was the one laughing at me. Felipe, Michael and I were getting close and I was really enjoying our time together.

The looks we got from the people were priceless. You could see all the thoughts running through their heads. You could see them whispering about the three of us. The next time I was taking pictures I got a lot of questions because everyone thought my role had changed. I told them all no because I was happy that my place was just with Michael.

Michael talked to Felipe about doing an erotic art show with him. Now I will say that there were not a lot of connections made from the first one except for Mandy, who was one of the models, and James, a photographer. I didn't really like the event the first time because mainly because of the photographer Michel worked with and that the show was in a house which I found odd...but anyway. Michael decided to work with this photographer again and do the erotic art show.

Michael, Felipe, Drake, and Fernando all went to the photo shoot. They were there all day and that night Michael, Felipe and I were supposed to go out that night. When Felipe brought Michael home he told me that he didn't feel good. I told him we would cancel the group date night that night. He said no that he just needed to rest for a bit. After he threw-up he went to go lay down. This scared me because I was worried about his medication might be making him sick. I woke him up and gave him a piece of bread so he could take his pill because I didn't want him taking it on an empty stomach. I would have just let him sleep the rest of the night but he told me to wake him up in 2 hours so I did with soup. I asked him how he was feeling and he said he was feeling better. As we continued to talk I figured out why he was sick...he had been drinking out in the sun all day long. I was pissed. I was so worried since he got home and here I was worried for nothing. I took the bowl of soup back and told him if he wanted it he could get it himself.

Felipe was mad that I told him that he should have stopped him from drinking so much. Felipe didn't feel it was his place. I understand that but this was a bit different in my eyes. He and Michael were developing a relationship and because of this there is a certain type of friendship Felipe had to develop with me. I know that if I had been there I wouldn't have let Michael drink so much knowing he was still early in taking his medication and so far we had been lucky there were no side effects. When Felipe went out with him because I had asked him to watch him when they were out I was hoping that he would have thought of this and told him to slow down because he had not eaten. In my eyes when you are in a relationship you watch out for each other and I would have told Michael that he had not eaten, was in the sun and about his medication which would have slowed Michael down.

We all went on the date night. I had a good time with Michael but Felipe was still mad. I couldn't get Felipe to really dance with us. I had moved on...I had said my piece and was over it. We were out to have a good time together. I am the type of person once I have said what I needed to say and let you say what you need to say...and we talk...I'm done. The night didn't go well and as it turned out this was the last time we all did a group date night.

The first erotic art show Michael did with the photographer he didn't get any of the pictures and that is all he wanted as payment for doing the show and the photo shoot. This time he did 2 photo sessions with this photographer...the one I just told you about...and one with Prime. The only pictures Michael liked were his idea with Prime. So the photographer agreed to give Michael all the pictures he wanted as payment for allowing him to use the pictures in the show...so they did the show. The day of the show it was a mess...1st the photographer didn't bring the memory card or flash drive like he said he would with the pictures...2nd the photographer was drunk and didn't stay and promote his work so that the guys made money off his work because they got a portion of the sale price...3rd we forgot Michael's medication and Felipe was nice enough to go back to the house and get it...4th the number that Prime did with Opal (the one they had just done at the show) got messed up because people wouldn't move out of the way...5th the guys were supposed to get a portion of the tips and wouldn't have gotten any of that if I had not went up to the owner with the tip jar saying do you want me to split this up with the guys because the last show the jar disappeared before the end of the night. We did get to see Maria again and as usually she was her bubble self. Felipe and Michael wore a pair of wings she made to sell at the show. That night she mentioned to us that she was starting her own wing designs and wanted to do a show and would contact Michael with the details when she knew them.

Michael didn't have time to worry about that because he had a show coming up. Michael made shirts for all the guys to wear during the opening number so they looked more like a group. I will say the shirts were cool. We went and bought iron-ones of letters and dragons to put on the shirts for the guys. He gave Felipe's his one night when he came down and he gave the rest to the guys the night of the show. Michael thought he would try a different type of opening number this time for the show. "Ladies and Gentleman" by Saliva was the song he chose and figured he would do the first part and the guys would come out one at a time to introduce them to the crowd. Fantasy was just around the corner.

Michael knew the guys he was taking…had the music and was ready to do a male revue show at Fantasy. Felipe, Prime, Fernando, the Canadian and his cousin Baby Face went to this messed up show. Now the bar itself was very large with 3 bars in on. The first was more like a sports bar and was smaller. It had a lot of T.V's and a smaller bar with a lot of seating but no dance floor. The next bar was bigger with pool tables and a pretty big bar…I would say this was the main bar. There were doors along one wall that lead outside to a very nice seating area with a pool. This part of the bar was where you could find the Canadian if you were looking for him. The area where we did the show didn't have a stage but the dressing rooms and small entryway lead right out to the dance floor…which was nice. Now the show itself was messed up for several reasons. The first reason…if you remember the dancers that I talked about before with the ego size attitudes without purpose…well they were one of the problems. First the dancers told everybody they knew not to come to the lame show we were having but to come see their show they were going to do at our half time. Next they and the drag queens kept coming back to where we were getting dressed drinking, being loud and walking into the closed dressing room and doing drugs…you could tell this by the behaviors they exhibited when they came out. They were a piece of work. I didn't have much to do with them but if their heads were any bigger they would have floated away. During the half time of the show we all walked outside to smoke when one of the other dancers friends asked me why I wasn't inside taking pictures of the dancers and I just replied that I would wait till the really hot professional dancers returned to the stage before I took any more pictures. Yes I just smiled and turned my head…oh well…yes I can be a bit snarky if you say something off color to me or put my guys down.

So that was the first problem…now the second… We have all our music on one IPod, except Felipe he never gives us his music. The list tells them who is dancing to what songs, when to pause the music so Michael can speak, what song needed to be repeated for the hot seat, when to switch IPods for Felipe and a lay out of the show. The one that hired us and the DJ kept messing up the music. How hard is it to read a list and to work an IPod? Yea I didn't think it was that hard but maybe that is for some people. The whole night I was running back upstairs to fix their mistakes with the IPod.

The show was great. The first part of the show went great and everyone that showed up had a blast. I sat with a wonderful man who was their taking pictures too. I didn't know at the time but he would be one of the Boyz biggest fans and even put them in a world-wide blog he writes about male dancers. There was also one gentleman that I talked to told me that my Boyz were the nicest, sweetest, amazing looking men he had ever seen… then he went on to say that he had been to other shows but because of his size nobody ever came up to him but they did and he would always be a fan. I thought that was so nice of him to say. I will say that the guys do not care who you are, what you look like, male, female, green, purple, or pink when you come to see them you will get attention because they all care about other people and they want everyone who comes to see them to have a good time. Well this gentleman played the shots game during the show. That is where 4 – 5 guys sit down in chairs and hold a shot glass between their legs and you have to do the shot without using your hands. Now the person with the most creative way wins by vote of the crowd. Well Michael picked him to be part of the game. Now he was not the most creative but when he tipped his head back he lost his balance and fell over…BUT…never lost the shot glass and didn't spill a drop. Everyone can appreciate a man that can handle a shot so he won. He was a fan he came to a few shows after that and even brought a crowd with him. He has moved away now so he can't come to the shows but he still talks to Michael sometimes and he still follows the Boyz.

The end of the night the Canadian decided he was not ready to go to sleep. Fernando ended up sharing a room with him and was not happy with that. Although we offered for him to sleep in our room but he smiled and said no he would just tough it out…Yea…that is what we thought too. Anyway, we had to take Fernando back to the hotel because when we walked out of the gas station from getting some food since there was not anything around we saw the Canadian still over in the bar parking lot talking to the guys he had picked up at the bar because they had drugs. He drove down the road and told Fernando that he would meet him back at the hotel.

Now the car ride home was quiet so we don't really know what happened in the other room...except that the guys that the Canadian invited over stayed for a bit. The Canadian was bouncing off the wall according to Fernando. When I reminded him that I told him he could have come to our room he just smiled and said that he was fine. Yea...I was thinking the same thing but one may never know.

At home things were ok. Michael began to exhibit behaviors I was not happy with. He would say things like he didn't want anyone to depend on him not even his family. He wished he could just disappear. He started talking to Felipe in secret...which some of the conversations I understood because they were about sex and stuff and Michael didn't want to throw it in my face...but just the odd texts. It is hard to explain but when you know Michael and know the way he is...him acting soft or needy and all cute and cuddly...it is odd.

Michael had come down with these small bumps on his feet that hurt him when he had to walk or stand for any length of time. We tried everything to get rid of them but nothing worked. He would pop the little blisters and it would help for the moment but they would come back and worse. We were lost and had no idea what to do or how to fix the problem. One day our car stopped working and he had to walk to work which sent him into a downward spiral. This went on for about 2 weeks. The stuff on his feet made it very hard to walk and then standing on them for 8 hours he was in real pain. Felipe drove down several times to get him from work so he didn't have to walk...see told ya he was a sweetheart. He even got a ticket one of those times. Now Michael has never been a happy thinking person but this was different. Everything and everyone was against him and he hated the world.

Felipe showed up one day and told us to tow the car and he paid to have it fixed. I thanked him very much for this because we didn't have the money but we had been without a car before and as a family made it through it. As a family we had always made it through anything life threw at us. He depended on me and me on him...always. Now he seemed to depend on not us but Felipe. This behavior was not like him. I chalked it up to the illness but he needed to get out of the mood he was in. He stopped being the strong man I married and it made me worried. He lost his job because of all the time off he had to use going to the doctor and just missing work. He wasn't looking for job either. When I would mention this to him that I needed help with the bills and the family...trying to get him back to where he was...my husband and the father of our kids...he would only say he would and then I would never see it.

The littlest thing would send him back into a downward spiral. I know learning you have HIV is scary and worrying about giving it to the one you love or your buddy was hard on him. When we lost our twins I went to a very dark place and Michael got me out of it. He told me the truth of what was going on and it shook me back to reality. The dark place lasted about a year and we were almost at 7 months since we found out he had this disease. Now losing children is extremely hard and I had to finish out my pregnancy since I was so far along and I knew what it was like to have kids since we had two so this was devastating. I am not saying that what Michel learned was not devastating because it was but like he and I knew...he brought it on himself by the choices he made. I needed my husband back...I needed to save him like he did me for us and our kids.

Felipe came down one time when Michael was at work and we talked about this and Felipe understood but after our talk I never saw any behavior changes. I never came right out and said all the stuff I was thinking because Michael and I are private people and I didn't want Felipe to think badly about Michael for the things I was thinking but because I didn't see any changes on Felipe's side I was going to have to do it all on my own. I realized this when I found out that Felipe decided not to stay covered to finish one time, during sex. Just to say that was a bullshit move that pissed me off like no other.

Ok...remember we were dancing at Sidewinders every Friday now... well this Friday Michael had a new guy showing up. Michael had met him on one of the hook-up sites...he got on them for obvious reasons but to also look for dancers. It so happened that he began to talk to a guy who was a nursing student. The first time I met him I thought he had an explosive personality. He was very friendly, well built and very handsome. He was also very intelligent and easy to talk to. There was something that took me by surprise though. You know how someone's voice just doesn't fit them... well Clint had a higher pitched voice than I expected. He also did this thing when he would say "Yea"...he would lift one shoulder and tilt his head towards it. It was cute. He was already a model for a well-known major underwear company. The underwear company he worked for was having a contest for new models. Michael told Prime he should try out. Now most of the models they had were nowhere near as well built as Prime.

Clint went over well when he danced at Sidewinders. The next time he danced we were at Chris's and he went over well then too so Michael welcomed him to the group. I liked Clint he was very funny...his humor was a bit dry like mine so I liked it. He had a boyfriend and he told me he was a doctor. That wasn't surprising for me because it makes since he would be a nurse since his boyfriend was a doctor.

With all the things I see during a show and on weekends allows me to get some interesting pictures. When the Boyz dance on the weekend it is always a lot of fun hanging out. Unfortunately it is a trial and error trying to get those amazing shots that Michael posts on his Facebook pages. I got an amazing picture of Michael and Felipe on Memorial Day weekend along with many other pictures of the Boyz on other weekends. I will say I could make a whole video of pictures and video of Felipe and call it the many faces of Felipe filled with all the odd faces and funny dances...Hunter... for example...is hard to photograph because he moves around so much... Drake always likes to make faces when he sees that I am taking pictures... the Canadian...well...there is something about the tone of his skin that just doesn't photograph well because he always looks washed out...Michael would always put his arms up which made it hard to get his face. Speaking of pictures when we got back from the show Michael and I decided that it was time to make a video for the group. I had enough pics and videos from Chris's, Sidewinders, and shows. Now for those of you who do not make video's let me tell you that it is not just simple task. You have to pic the song...cut and edit all the video's you're going to use...find the pictures and edit them...place all those in an order that looks good...sends the message you are wanting to say...make sure it all flows together...make sure on different parts of the song you have the right pictures or video...yea not easy.

I picked Timebomb by Kyle Minogue and the video was a big hit. I picked that song because that is mine and Michael's song. Every time it plays we dance no matter what he is doing. We don't dance with anyone else during that song and during that song no one can pull us apart. There have been a few that have tried but failed...and I don't dance with anyone... except the other dancers if I can't find Michael.

Now what was going on at home was different. It had been 8 or 9 months since we had found out Michael had HIV. Michael was acting very oddly depressed. I had given him space and time to deal with everything just like he did me with the twins but it was time to get up off the mat and deal with the reality of our...well his...situation. Michael couldn't seem to do this on his own so like he helped me it was my turn to help him. The events of one day made my mind up for me and from that point on I was going to get Michael back to where he needed to be.

One afternoon Felipe was supposed to come down but Michael told me to text him and tell him not to come down. Michael went into the bedroom and wanted to be alone. This behavior scared me. I went in the bedroom to check on him but he said he wanted to be alone and asked me to leave. I went and sat on the couch and said prayers. I felt the urge to go back to the bedroom. I went and knocked on the door. When Michael came to the door he looked like he had been crying but he also had a certain sadness and indescribable look and air about him. He asked for the phone and went to the bathroom. I went in the bedroom and waited for him to come out of the bathroom. When he came back into the room he told me that he was contemplating suicide; had the knife out and everything. I didn't know what to think all I knew is that he was still here and I wanted to talk to him I wanted to hold him. Then he told me that Felipe was coming down to get him.

I told him I didn't want him to go. He had just told me that I had almost lost him and he wanted to leave. I wanted to help him through what he was feeling. He needed out. This really hurt me. He left me crying in the bedroom. I did not know how long they would be gone or what was going on. I was lost; I felt abandoned. We were a team. It was him and I against the world. With Michael not being the Michael I married I had no idea where his head was. I knew Felipe was really falling for Michael. He wanted way more time alone with him which caused a bit of problem. Our youngest daughter had noticed the two of them and I told Michael about it so they didn't sit by each other anymore. I could just feel disaster because of the behavior. How was this going to end? I knew Michael was never going to leave but I felt there was going to be some odd ultimatum from Michael about Felipe being around somehow?

You know I was fighting an uneven fight. Michael and I had a past that was filled with some beautiful and wonderful memories but unfortunately there were some very horrible things too. Then we had kids, bills, we were dealing with his bi thing, all the past and present lies, the clients all this was in our present time which is a lot. Felipe had nothing but a good time. I had all these things to get Michael through and Felipe was an unexplored open road with no bumps. Now Felipe did things that aggravated Michael but Michael wouldn't really tell him nor do anything about it.

Michael had Felipe who could come and go as he wanted. He didn't have to worry about kids to keep one of them home. Felipe had money because he didn't have really anything to pay for so they had money to spend. Felipe was free as a bird. With Michael's outlook...because of the illness...this is what he was looking for. Not looking for but what he wanted for himself. Like I said before he didn't want anyone to depend on him so the thought of freedom was appealing. I understood that. At this point the grass did look greener on the other side. I know it wouldn't be and Michael would not be happy in the long run but in his state of mind I wasn't sure. I knew if he did leave we would be done. I know Michael would eventually come to his senses but if he left we would be done. I wouldn't have taken him back when he made the realization of his mistake. My biggest fear was the lingering ultimatum I felt Michael was going to give me about Felipe. Felipe being around all the time was a worry. I didn't mind Felipe coming around but I didn't want to share every aspect of my life with Michael with Felipe. I really needed Michael back to where he was.

When Michael came home I was relived. Felipe didn't come in this time so it was just Michael and I. Michael walked in the bedroom where I was laying down and gave me a kiss and handed me a present...it was a Maleficent bobble head. Michael said he was thinking of me and saw it and just had to get it for me because he knew she is my all-time favorite character. I was glad to hear he was thinking of me because he was all I was thinking of. The behavior between Michael and Felipe continued down a very odd path.

The text the two would send each other began to include words like baby and honey towards each other. Now these are words people use towards each other when they are in a relationship. I was still trying to navigate through his first real "gay relationship" and the illness at the same time.

Yes fish out of water again. See...I only understand what those words hold because of the relationship I am in. I only understand what I know where as Michael sees things different. Just like the guy off the show "Friends" would say "hey" one way when he was hitting on a chick but can just be said "hey". So words mean one thing to me and another to Michael. Just like my all-time most hated word...Daddy. To me it means the father of my kids not something sexual which is the way it is said in the gay world. So things are different and I understand that but when it came to the two of them I questioned things...mainly because of the way Michael was acting.

I found this cute little saying and I showed Michael and told him that was to him and gave him a kiss on the cheek. The saying went something like...I would fight a bear for you well like a care bear. Without missing a beat he asked if he could send it to Felipe. Really he didn't really say anything to me but had to send it to him. I said I didn't care because it was no longer important to me. It was stuff like that that bothered me. This was so out of character for Michael. Not that Michael would have made a big deal anyway but he would have given me a kiss or said that was cute... something to give me attention. I was reaching out to him but he was only thinking of himself. He wanted to send that to Felipe so show him he was thinking of him...HELLO what did he think I was doing? We were not alone anymore because Felipe had crawled into a spot which I was not comfortable with because the behaviors were out of the normal for Michael. Michael was beginning to depend on Felipe for support and wanted to make sure Felipe knew he cared which was fine especially after all Felipe had done for him and us but this seemed like something else. Michael had become what I call soft. What I mean by that is that he is kind of a loner who doesn't show a lot of affection towards anyone...or need anyone...we both walk together by each other. Yes...we support each other...when needed...but neither of us needs it that often. I was not even really needy when I lost the twins I just sometimes became a bitch and very distant.

Michael needed to stand on his own two feet. He needed to come out of his funk. HIV wouldn't kill him he would just have to take medication the rest of his life. The illness would interfere with things but it could be overcome. We needed to be a family again, just the family. It needed to go back to where...Michael stood on his own two feet...be with his family... and be with whomever without all the soft needy stuff because that wasn't

Michael. I was going to help Michael see that because that is what he did for me. Michael was shrinking away. The man I loved was disappearing and turning into someone who was softer and dependent on others instead of the strong personality I married. He stopped being my Zeus. I am glad I decided to help my husband get back to where he needed to be. I didn't want to hurt Felipe because I cared about him too but he was part of the problem through no fault of his own.

Michael had done the same for me when we lost the twins. I couldn't see the end of the tunnel and Michael helped me. I have always thanked him for that. He didn't have an easy time of it but in the long run it helped us get back to our marriage. This is what I needed to do for Michael. He needed to regain his focus. He needed to get his compass back and I was going to help him. Now I might add this was not going to be easy. I had to figure out how to get Michael to stand on his own without Felipe around… and by myself without Michael figuring it out.

Here were these two men who did care about each other but it was more of a destructive type relationship for Michael. Felipe had begun to talk about his past and realize some of his behaviors today steamed from his past. Michael made him realize he really needed to stand on his own two feet and not let people take advantage of him. Felipe needed someone who would call him on his shit and not let him get by with hiding inside himself by not facing reality…even though it pissed Felipe off…he needed this and Michael did this. The catch 22 at the time is Felipe wanted someone to take care of him too…someone who would be around whenever he wanted them…Michael couldn't do that…he had his family…which was not fair to Felipe. Michael was willing to do this because of his state of mind at the time. Michael would have had Felipe down every night…would have went anywhere Felipe wanted him to go…Michael would have done anything because it got him out of the house and away from his responsibilities. Michael was in an odd place right now…he had changed and not in a good way since he had found out he was infected. He wanted someone to take care of him but at the same time he wanted left alone…it was a confusing time. Michael walks beside his partners and Michael was not doing that now.

For me Felipe had become part of my life. He helped me and my family emotionally and financially without missing a beat…without wanting anything in return but our thanks. He was there every time we needed him and I loved him for that…especially since Michael had lost his job and wasn't looking for another. He honestly cared without asking for anything. I remember one time he and I were lying on the bed and he…just like a puppy…rolled on his back wanting his belly rubbed. I loved his hugs because they always made me feel better. He let me cry and told me things would be ok. He was there with the family…held the grandbaby…even helped put her to sleep. He could make me smile…when there was not a lot to smile about sometimes. I loved to watch him laugh and smile when I would pick on him…I know he didn't always like it but he dealt with it like a champ. He would let me talk to him about Michael and never tell Michael. He was part of my family and I loved him and now I could only hope that the two would make it through what I was about to do. If Felipe could just hold on till I got Michael back to where he was when they first met we would be great.

One thing I did was our date nights went back to just being us and nobody else. On our date nights Felipe could not be dancing because it was our night and the focus needed to be on us. Michael scheduled the guys to dance so that should not have been a problem. Well, it happened anyway. Michael and I had a great night together on our first date night between just the two of us in a long time. We were ready to go but Michael needed to talk to Felipe so he went to the back where all the guys were getting ready to leave. When he came out he told me that Felipe wanted to walk out with us…by itself…no big deal…but because of what I was trying to do and the fact that it was our date night and Michael had Felipe dancing… even though I asked him not to…it was a big deal. We waited for Felipe to gather his things to walk out with us. As we reached the car I heard Michael tell Felipe he loved him. I stopped dead in my tracks.

I knew that Michael had told me that he had "a type of" love for Felipe. The way Michael explained it to me was with how Army buddies develop a close tight relationship for each other because of the experiences they had together or like Sam and Frodo in Lord of the Rings…he always added… not like the way I love you…and I understood that. The difference between them and Michael and Felipe is that the army buddies and Sam and Frodo don't have sex. Sex added closeness and an intimacy to their relationship just like it does to every relationship. I know that Michael had just been through a terrible time and Felipe had stayed so he was just not a toy but to say it out loud like that told me something else especially with me standing there. Michael was comfortable being in the spot he was in with the two of us and changing was not something he wanted to do.

Well that night I told Michael that I was not happy with that and he got bent saying fine I tried to have a good night but I give up because nothing makes you happy because you heard me say that it ruined your whole night. Can you say drama queen? I had no idea that me expressing the fact that it was our night and we didn't need to walk a grown man outside but that we did and then you say you love him and that I was angry about it would piss you off so much…Really. Yea…this was going to be hard.

I knew Michael loved his family…I knew Michael needed Felipe around…and we needed to find a healthy balance like it was in the beginning. This was going to be hard for me to help Michael find a healthy balance because Michael would slip back to the Michael I didn't know quickly. I was glad Michael had the Boyz to focus on.

CHAPTER 15

Mandy, the girl we met at the erotic art show called Michael and wanted help with her first show. Mandy is a mother of two with dark hair…now… her personality doesn't match her size. She only stands about 5'5" but her personality makes her 7'. I didn't really know her at this time but I found out the more time I spent with her that she is a wonderful woman. She asked Michael for 3 men for her show. Michael picked Prime and Felipe to do the show with him. I agreed because the three of them were the biggest built guys, besides Drake, with the best bodies and they could do it. Felipe had really worked on getting himself thinner. He had once been heavy but he was looking really good.

She told them they needed to be there by 6. Unfortunately they didn't go on till 11. There was a lot of standing around doing nothing. Michael told me that all the girls that were there were very catty towards each other. Mandy had some beautiful wings to show to the crowd and the pictures I saw the guys looked great. I didn't get to go I was working. The only thing that came out of the day was Michael decided he was going to make the next girls group.

Mandy, who wanted to get back into modeling, sent out a message to all the models she knew about what Michael wanted to do and the response was great. Michael set up a day and time to talk to all the girls that were coming. Mandy told him that there were 20 girls who wanted to talk to him. Unfortunately when he showed up there was only 1…Sin. She was a full figured burlesque performer who could sing and she dyed her hair making her look like Marilyn Monroe. Her personality was warm and friendly but

168

larger than any room she was in. She was a mother of 6 who had just recently got into performing and she was interested in working for Michael. She had the same beliefs as Michael...or so we thought. Michael is all about the show and wants everything to go off beautifully and she is like that too but is a bit chaotic. She has big dreams but you could tell she had just started and didn't put a lot of thinking in things. A lot of her performances are just winged...not a lot of practice. Her performances were amazing though... she is one that can do that...imagine how great they would be if she were to practice...and her voice is like a dream. She has big dreams but she is not a planner or how the nitty gritty stuff needs to be done. Michael is kind of like that but that is what he has me for.

At this time Michael started talking to Superman, the only nice and well-built dancer from Fantasy, about dancing with us. Superman was all for it. Michael told him that he would keep him in mind for our next show. Michael knew he would fit in well and would be a great asset to the group.

Michael needed someone to help us out when Opal couldn't go with us and perform. Sin wanted the job and was eager to begin working. She began to talk to Michael because burlesque performers do not make that much money. Something else I noticed because I had met some of the burlesque performers they were defiantly not the Pussycat Dolls. These performers thought they were though but when you take away the fun house mirror they are looking through they are really a poster child for eaters anonymous or denture cream. Well at least some of the ones where we live.

Their beliefs have been fed by the fans. Where we live people who go to shows applauded because they got up there and performed no matter what they look like. It is not that they wouldn't rather see the Pussycat Dolls but they applaud these performers for their efforts. This behavior gives them a false sense of reality because if they really looked at themselves they wouldn't be up there performing. I know this makes me sound cold but we all know what we want to see and they are not it. They are just the only thing people can hire. I do not hate overweight and older people but let's be realistic. If you are heavy or older don't act like you are a sex kitten unless you are playing on the fact that you are overweight or older. The other groups are the ones that are not attractive or there is not a spot on them that is not covered with pictures or words and their performing skill remind me of a kindergarten class performance. I just know that I do not want to see this and most don't. I wouldn't want pity applause from anyone. I would want them to enjoy seeing me. The entertainment world is cold and cruel. We created this world though and sadly who would you rather see performing, honestly?

So the meeting went well with Sin and she was very eager to start up with the group. Our next show though Opal was able to do with us. Well if you want to call what was about to happen a show. Now I had talked on Facebook with the drag queen putting on the show. Now remember when I talked about some drag queens...well I am going to just tell you what happened and let you make up your own mind. So we get hired for a two day event. The two day event was for her birthday. The first night we are supposed to do a show at a birthday party and the next night we are supposed to gogo at a bar that was in the area...which was also a birthday celebration for her. This area is known as Shitville because of the experience. Ok so let me set the scene for you so you can get a complete picture of the whole two days.

We pull up to this broke down 1950's looking hotel out in the middle of nowhere with a big empty field on one side. When I got out of the car I said to the group...wonder how many bodies are buried out there? Everyone thought that was funny. It was not so funny when we walked inside the hotel. Now the comment was not so funny because it could have been true. It was the hottest two days out of the year with a heat index of around 115 degrees.

So when we walked into the hotel it was hot and had an odd smell which was nothing compared to the room. With the heat being this bad you cannot imagine the smell. Walking down the hall there was a woman who said don't worry I paid for the room for an hour. I thought I knew then what we were in for but I was still not completely fully aware of what was to come. When you walked into our room it was a sauna because you immediately started sweating. Now Prime had some health issues due to his workout routine and not being able to sleep very well so imagine what the heat was doing to him. He looked so drained and white as a ghost. I told them all I would walk down and talk to someone at the desk. When I walked by the bathroom I noticed that all we had were hand towels and Prime wanted to take a shower.

When I got to the desk this short and angry Asian man came to the counter and asked what I wanted in very broken English. I told him that the air conditioner must be broken because it was a sauna and we didn't have any towels. He then proceeded to yell, "Did you steal my towels"...accusing me of stealing the towels out of the room when we had just got there. I told him that we just got here and I wanted towels for the room and the air fixed. He put a towel on the counter and I told him there were four of us and I wanted more. Without missing a beat, "You better not steal my towels" all the while giving me a dirty look and grabbed a few more towels and took off to our room with me following him.

When he got there he told us it was working. Prime told him that if it didn't get cooler that we wanted to switch to another room. The guy just looked at him and said, "You be fine" and left. This set Prime off and I don't blame him. He was sweeting and that was not good in his condition. He seemed to be getting whiter with every second. He is a trooper because even though he didn't feel good he understands the show must go on. This dump was the worst we had ever stayed in. Opal and Cassy went with us so I went over to their room to put on my make-up because as soon as I started to put it on in our room it was sliding back off. I noticed that there appeared to be blood on the floor between their beds.

Now this should have told us we were in trouble but like good little entertainers we marched on and just joked about it. Opal got into her first drag outfit she was going to wear in the show. The guys all took showers and got ready to go and we left for the event. The bar was nice inside and because it was a college town it was wall to wall young people inside. This usually means tips will not be good...they like to talk and touch but keep the money to themselves.

When we got there we were shown where we would be getting dressed. The bar had a small upstairs room they used for VIP people, I guess. The room upstairs was small but it was enough room for all of us to have our own little space. The event though was going to be outside in the heat and the drag queen who hired us had not even finished setting up or was not finished getting ready herself. She was a loud, full size dramatic black man who stood about 6'6". Another problem was that the guys had to walk through the bar to get to the area where they would be performing in the heat. Michael went down stairs to talk to the drag queen and see when she wanted them to get started. When Michael came back upstairs I knew something was wrong. He walked over to me and said you handle it…please. See I know my husband well enough that when he wants me to handle it… the bitch needs to come out because it is not going well. Michael and I both would rather people get mad at me then him because he can always say he will talk to me but they just won't hire Michael again if they get mad at him.

I went downstairs to get the details. The show we perform is already written out and we even have all our music on an IPod so we are pretty much set up. Well, that was not what we were doing. Instead she had hired us to walk around and be eye candy, take pictures with her, take pictures with her guests and put on a fake sword fight. As she began to explain this to me I told her that was not the show we had talked about. She asked me did I think that we could do this instead but that she would still pay us what we agreed upon. I had read all the conversations and been part of the conversation between them and I know Michael had explained our show to her. If she wanted to pay us to do a show but not actually do a show then it was fine by me but I wanted paid because that was not what we had talked about or set up. I said sure. I asked her what she wanted Opal to do and was told that she didn't need another drag queen. I went back upstairs to explain it to the guys and to Opal.

I explained they were all still getting paid but it was not a show we were doing and I explained what she wanted. Good news for them because they really did not have to do anything. I explained how she wanted them to come out and in what order. Once they were out there I explained what she wanted them to do. This didn't work though because the way she told me never happened. Nothing went the way it was supposed to because of her but whatever. I looked at Opal and told her that she had the night off and we would still pay her and that we were sorry. She is such a trooper because she said no problem and hung out anyway to talk with the guys and help me take pictures. Well she was supposed to because the drag queen had said that room was for private dances and if they wanted their pictures taken with the Boyz that all pictures would be done up in the room. That never happened either.

The event was more like a small catered birthday party. There was a game that night and because it was a college town and the team lost not a lot of people showed up. It went on for about 3 hours. After it was over I walked up to the drag queen to get our pay. She began to tell me that she thought that the price had changed since we did not do the show. I told her no. Then came the drama and let me tell you it was drama. She told me she was discounting all the stuff she had bought and I told her no because we did not use any of it she could take it back.

Now I had to listen to her complain about paying us but I didn't care. I wanted our money. When she got back from the ATM she was short. I was pissed and said I needed it all. She told me that she would give the rest of it to me tomorrow because it was her show we were dancing for the next night too. Thank goodness that the bar was paying for us that night. I did not want to but I had no choice.

I went back and told Michael and now he was even madder at the situation then he was before. Opal and Cassy had to leave because they were doing a rodeo the next day so we paid them and they left. The Canadian, who had tried to sneak alcohol earlier, asked Michael if he could take off but promised he would be back the next day for the gogo event and Michael said yes. That was against my better judgment but whatever he is considered an adult by law so...whatever.

The rest of us were tired, hot and hungry. Now I know I cannot name this fast food restaurant but like a queen that wears a crown this is where we went. We were ordering 2 double big burgers with cheese meals and on the screen it showed the small burgers. I told Felipe to make sure she knew that because that is not what we wanted. The lady said she understood but the screen never changed. Now we told her this 3 times and each time she said she understood but the screen never changed so we pulled around.

When we got to the window she handed us drinks that were sitting by the window but they were wrong so we gave them back. She just put them back up on the counter, took out the straws and handed us different ones...can you say YUK. So when we got our food we knew immediately that the burgers were wrong. Bet you didn't see that coming. Felipe knocked on the window and when she finally came to the window he explained to her that he had told her 4 times during the time he was ordering that they were double big cheese burger and that he was missing his chicken tenders. Standing there with no emotion on her face she said wait a minute turned shutting the window and walking over to what I can only assume was her boss but I can tell ya she is no boss I would want to work for because of the look on her face. When the lady came to the window she opened it up and simply said no while shutting the window and walked away. Now I know what you're thinking right now...WTF are you serious. We were in shock. All of us kind of just said at the same time...did she just say no and walk away...WTF. We were in disbelief. After sitting there in the drive-thru for several minutes waiting for her to come back Michael just said fuck it lets just go. I will tell you that when we got back home I called the headquarters of this fast food chain and they took care of it by sending me a coupon for a free burger...1 free burger...yea like that would have made up for the BS of the night. I will never eat there again.

We all just went back to the hotel. Michael and I took the other room because we were the only smokers and yes this hotel was so old that you could still smoke in the room. So now let me add this, remember when I said their room had blood stains on the floor well the path lead right under my bed. Yes, I did not lift the mattress because I was afraid that I was sleeping on the mattress covering up the dead hooker. Felipe was use to staying with us in our room but tonight we went to the other room...I guess he complained to Michael because Michael told me when we got home Felipe was hurt we went to the other room. For me though...I wanted my own bed so that I could stretch out. As the only girl in a group of men I slept with my bra on and now because it was just me and Michael in the room I could take it off...yea me. I was also happy I could have the TV on for noise since I didn't have my fan. Michael was happy too because he could stretch out and know I wouldn't touch his foot while I was sleeping. We could raise his foot up and put ice on it...which made him happy. He was having such a hard time with it. His foot had become so swollen and hurt to walk on. We had iced it in the car and he kept it elevated as much as he could but the show must go on ... which meant he had not put it up for about 4 hours. By this time Michael had developed a 50 cent size bump on the side of his foot because we had finally made it to the doctor and they had gave him this cream and instead of getting rid of whatever it was it seemed to draw them out. So his foot would swell. We both were happy we could just be in our beds and smoke while we were relaxing. Michael and I laughed about the night and the BS that went on that night and trust me there was a lot to choose from.

If that night was not bad enough…at 11am the phone rang. Now we were told that we had 2 rooms for 1 day and 1 of those rooms for 2 days. The clerk at the desk asked us if we were staying again and when I told her yes she asked if we could come down and pay for the room then. I told her it was already supposed to be paid for because one of the rooms was supposed to be for 2 nights. The clerk said sorry but that she did not have the room booked for two nights. I asked her if she could give me a bit of time so that I could figure things out. I began to call the drag queen.

The drag queen told me that she told Michael that she was paying for the first night but the bar was paying for the second. I told her that the room was supposed to already be paid for before we left and that is what she had told us. She told me that she told Michael that the bar was supposed to take care of the other room and that she didn't have anything to do with that. I finally told her that I was Michael's wife and some of the conversations she was having on the computer was with me and that she needed to get something figured out and let me know because she told us the rooms were taken care of before we left. Her stunned silence was not very reassuring. She finally said that she would get in touch with the bar and get back to us. When I hung up I told everyone and nobody was very happy. When she called back she gave us wonderful news.

She told us that the bar never said they agreed to pay and that she didn't have the money but we could hang down at her house. We were all so thrilled and yes that was written with as much sarcasm as possible. Now came the time to tell everyone. Prime was still not feeling well but we loaded everything up and headed into town to find something to eat. Trust me we did not go to that crappy crown place.

This town looked even worse in the daytime. Nobody believed in cool air or cleanliness. We all sat around bitching because we didn't want to go to her house but we were running out of options. Prime was not feeling well and needed to lay down somewhere cool. We texted the Canadian to see where he was and if he wanted to go out there with us…but he didn't answer. This did not surprise me since this was what I figured would happen. We all just bit the bullet and headed out to her house.

Her house was out in the middle of nowhere. Now remember I said the heat index was around 115 degrees…three of the hottest days of the year. As we walked into the house we realized that it felt hotter in her house than it did outside. At least outside you had somewhat of a breeze when it would blow. We all went downstairs because at least it was a few degrees cooler but we were uncomfortable from the second we walked in until we left. Prime was beginning to melt away…if he got any whiter I would have thought he was a ghost. The drag queen offered Prime a place to lie down. Now let me explain…it was a very small room with two twin beds and between them a coffee table with a bowl of condoms on it … Would you lay down?…Not me…no way. I followed her upstairs to ask her about our money when she looked at the thermostat and said, "Wow it is 90 degrees I guess I should turn on the air now". I wanted to scream at the top of my lungs…Duh Ya Think you stupid bitch…WTF!! I just smiled and said yea…it is very hot in here and proceeded to ask her about our money. She told me after I asked her about the money that I would get it tonight. This had to be the one of the worst days we have ever had on the road. It never did get cool in there but the prodigal son finally texted back so we all jumped at the chance to get in an air conditioned car for a bit and go get him.

Driving back to town we all thanked him because it was hot. Now the text we got from the Canadian made no sense. I had sent him a text asking him where he was and his reply was "heaven". The conversation went on but still made no sense. Prime was better at deciphering drunk so we all left but half way there he stopped talking. I told him that we would meet him at the bar where we had done the event. When we got there I waited at the car just in case he found the car and the guys all walked around. We waited for him for about an hour. Unfortunately we needed to get back to her house so we could attempt to get cleaned up for the show.

So that night the Boyz danced at the bar. Now to finish out this lovely story let me set up the bar. You know what a sewer plant smells like? Well there was one right beside the bar so you know what the bar smelled like. The cinder block building sat right beside a trailer park also so imagine the clientele. Now we went in and I sat at the bar waiting for the night to start. I ordered a drink which I never due during a show but after all I had been through I figured I deserved it and because I was afraid what the night had in store for us. On a side note … this goes out to Blake … the best bartender that works at the best bar for actually knowing how to fix a drink … CHEERS. I ordered a Margarita and I have never tasted anything so bad in my life it tasted like sprite with I have no idea what mixed in. I asked the bartender what I was drinking and when he answered and told me a Margarita I asked him if he was sure and he assured me that it was. I slid it back to him and asked for a coke. Which I should add that it tasted flat so I only had one that I sipped on all night and with each sip I wished I was home.

The Boyz had to share the small dressing room with drag queens which meant there was no room for them at all. I went back there once and was over powered by the smell of nasty perfume and body odor. I stayed out of the dressing room as much as possible. The night went well and the Boyz were popular. Even though we were down a dancer the bar thought we did such a good job he paid us the entire amount. We told him at the beginning we were taking off money because we were down a dancer but he liked what he saw. He was not a bad guy actually rather nice.

Now time to get the rest of my money from the drag queen. So when I pinned her down for the money after she acted like everything else was so important she handed me the money the bar had paid her, which was not enough. Then she starts pulling money out of her bra yes it was gross but I wanted my money. When it was all said and done she was short by $50. I told her we could take her to an ATM but she said she had no money in her bank. I knew then and there we were never going to get our money. She told us she would mail it to us within the week. Now you know as well as I do that I still, after all this time, still have not seen my money. Do you know a bit later she actually got a hold of us wanting us to work with her again...can you say...Hell No. So now what do you think about this type of drag queen? Sad to say this is not the only drag queen that has done this to the Boyz but that is another story for another time. So because we had no hotel room booked we had to drive home at 3:00am which is a 3 hour drive for us. When we got home almost on a daily basis we contacted the Canadian. Michael would text, call and Facebook him...nothing...no posts from him. We finally just started checking on his Facebook to see if anything changed...but nothing.

Now comes one of my favorite guys and he has actually become my brother. So, one night at Sidewinders a friend/fan of Michael brought us a new dancer...Raphael...Raph for short...said like the Ninja Turtles name, he is just as ornery. The 5'7" atomic bomb is on fire...who is just a country boy at heart. He sneaks up on ya and before you know it...you are in love with him. He has the most wonderful smile and laugh that time flies by when you are talking to him because he is so much fun to be around. That night, though, he was quiet and shy but I could see behind those beautiful blue/green eyes he was more…so much more. He didn't say much but his 1st outfit was a chainmail thong and a leather harness…quiet and shy my ass. That outfit doesn't go with quiet and shy. He had an odd way of dancing but it was his first night and I know he was nervous but under that dirty blonde hair I knew he loved it and was hooked. He did very well and he was very well received by everyone. Over the years he has become one of the family… to all of my family.

So Michael's foot was really bothering him and the bump was not going down but getting bigger. So Michael, Felipe and I were in the ER for Michael's foot when I got a message though our website. I contacted the person and they messaged me right back. I stepped outside to call them. Samantha, a stage name for a flamboyant eccentric drag queen whose outfits date back to the 70's and the wigs match the 80's the bigger the better. She was great and very excitable. She had seen a picture of the Boyz from the drag queen we will never work for again and wanted us to be the main event of her show. I spoke with her for about thirty minutes and told her to send me a date and we would be there.

When I got back into the room I told Michael and he was excited. It was another state for us. We were now going to be performing in 3 states. We were ready to get this show started. Michael and Felipe tried working on a group number but never could get together. Michael figured that they could use one of the opening numbers that they had used before. He let everyone know they had a show and to get their idea for a strip number together.

Michael took Fernando, Prime, Felipe, Superman and Opal…love ya girl. When we got to the venue it was not a bar instead it was a large room with a decent dance floor with a medium size stage at the far end a make-shift bar with tables sitting around. It was more like a banquet hall type place. Samantha had put up curtains for the group to get dressed behind. This venue had way more women than men which was fine as long as they enjoyed the show and tipped. When the show started you could tell they were ready to see half naked men. Before I start telling you about the show let me give all the women out there who go and see strippers a bit of advice… take a shower and clean up before you go. Men go down between your legs and they need to be able to breath…I am just saying…it is all on you and what you want them to say about you.

So the show started with a number between Michael, Felipe and Opal which went over very well. Then the Gogo boys went out and danced while Michael got ready for his strip. After his strip Michael came back and warned everyone not to breath when they went down on any of the women because the smell would make you pass out. Now that night Prime and Opal did a teaser number to the song, I Touch Myself, before the break that drove the woman nuts. As Opal sang Prime was on the stage dressed as a construction worker. He acted like he was just coming home from work and changing clothes. He slowly started to take off his hat, then his tool belt, stretching and rubbing his muscles as he went. Then he took off his shirt slowly and just as the song ended he had unbuttoned his pants and started to unzip them. Let's just say the ladies in the crowd were all ready to see the rest…but as it was just a teaser number he stopped.

The comment I made for all the ladies above I should also add a thank you to all of them because if it was not for the way they brought themselves to the show the group wouldn't have a funny story or I wouldn't have a great picture. Now it was Prime's turn to do his strip but he forgot what Michael had said to all of them. The face he made as he came up from between a girls leg…was priceless. His whole face was squished up like he had just smelled all of a sewer plant all at once. I just happened to be in the right spot for that picture. When he came to the back we all started laughing because I had showed everyone the picture. From that point on he said all women had tentacles between their legs and he would pull his hands up to his face and wave his fingers and hands around every time he made that comment.

Prime put on his black Spiderman costume which was very well made and Superman put on his costume that he had made and danced together. Many of the ladies wanted pictures with the super heroes. Not much happened that show as far as drama goes but it still had a few funny stories.

Michael had talked Prime into trying out for a contest with the underwear company Clint worked for. Prime seemed to be jumping through hoops to get votes to win the contest for the underwear company. The contest seemed to go forever. It was ridiculous. Prime's numbers were high which meant he was very popular. The sad part of all this were the comment on the pictures and videos. Most of them were great comments but some were just there to bitch. I only have one thing to say to someone who just spews hate like...you look stupid...SHUT UP!! When you say they are stupid pictures or how could someone let them be an object by showing all that skin...you look stupid because you are on the site looking at them... so what does that say about you. It is one thing to say to someone like the underwear you are wearing but they don't look good on you...or the color is not right for you...helpful criticism is good but just to be mean is spineless. The only reason you are blowing smoke is because you couldn't do what they are doing. If you could do better you would and if it is not your thing then why are you looking at the videos and pictures. Prime takes pride in what he does and tries very hard. When spineless people say things to him it really gets to him. We told him not to care about what those people say because they are not important they just want everyone to be as miserable as they are but Prime with his wonderful heart took it all to heart. This would be one of Primes' main problems which you will see later on.

Clint and Prime made some videos together for the company to post on the underwear site. The company sent 2 models to dance at Chris's with Prime and Clint. Michael and Drake danced that night too. I will say that they were very nice guys. Not as well-built as Prime, Drake, Michael and Clint but they were very nice guys. We all had a good time and I got some amazing pictures

Now the next weekend we heard what was supposed to have happened in the backroom. Bill, the D.J. at Chris's, told Michael that he caught Drake in the backroom on his knees with one of the underwear models. This is where we got the phrase "ish". That is when someone says they are straight but either 1 they are just denying things because they are not comfortable or 2 a couple of shots or drinks and they don't care. So if you ever hear me say "ish" you will know what we are talking about.

Now we heard again from our home away from home bar Rumors letting us know they wanted another show. This time we took Clint, Felipe, Superman, Prime and Sin, because Opal was having major back problems and had to stop. Now the drama of the night came from the girl Superman brought. Superman said she was a friend but she said she was his girlfriend...either way I wish she had never come because of the tension she caused. Superman's ex-girlfriend showed up with the guy who won the shot's game at Fantasy and the "whatever" she was girl told Superman that he couldn't go over to the side of the bar she was at. She is lucky I didn't hear her say that because I would have corrected her then but the tensions were running high and it was beginning to be felt by all. Michael, Felipe and Sin had a wonderful opening number which lead into Sin's strip number. She went over very well actually which was good since she was in a gay bar. This was the first time I actually heard Sin sing and wow Michael was right she was a very good singer. I noticed also that she knew how to pose for the best pictures...I wish she would teach that to the boys. Now back to the "whatever" girl...Superman came to me and told me he was missing out on money and when I asked why he explained. I told him to go where the money was and I would take care of the rest.

Well as soon as he headed over there she headed towards him but thank goodness she walked by me and I grabbed her arm and put her behind me. Now if someone would have done that to me I would have understood what that meant...but not her. I was taking more pictures when out of the corner of my eye I saw, working her way through the crowd on the other side of the room, she was headed right for him again with a look of disgust on her face. I headed right for her and got to her just before she made her way to him. I took ahold of her arm and told her to wait in the back for me I would be there in a minute.

I finished taking my pictures and walked to the back. She began bitching telling me that his ex-girlfriend had tried breaking them up and she was tired of it. She continued by saying that the ex-girlfriend was full of drama and she didn't want Superman around her. I let her rant for a second and then I told her that I didn't care. I finished by saying that during a show the guys were here to make money and as much money as they could and I didn't care if everyone out there wanted to sleep with him or if he had slept with everyone out there...he was single...so if you can't handle it then I didn't want to see her back out on the floor. She began to argue but I cut her off and said I don't care that is the way it was and I didn't care if she liked it or not. I know Superman heard an earful because he told me but he also told me that after she said her piece which was a different version than the truth he told her he would bring her over to me so we could talk about it... yea she said never mind and dropped the subject. The money he made that night made all the BS she was saying easier to listen to.

Sin had a lot of fun that night. She made more money than she had ever made before. The only thing I had a problem with was when there are other people out there trying to make money then she should have been in the back. I don't think she was used to working with a professional group but it was her first show so I let things slide. She played around with Clint and Prime a lot and the crowd liked that. The lesbians that came loved her personality.

When we got back home Tree Top contacted Michael and wanted us to do a show. Now we had wanted to do a show but it seemed nobody wanted to pay what we were worth…the price other bars pay because they make the money back and then some…because they are never disappointed. So Michael began to work out a show. Now while this was going on Prime had decided he was done jumping through hoops for this underwear company. They wanted him to do one more video. Michael told him that he should just do it because Michael knew Prime would win. So Prime talked to Michael about this one song and the idea he had for the song. Michael told him it would be great because it showed his personality and people would love it. He made the video and sent it to them…and instantly it was a hit. That weekend Prime danced with Clint.

It didn't go very well. I guess Prime and Clint had done a video that the underwear company wanted to post but Clint didn't want it to be posted. The company talked to Prime and asked him to talk to Clint so they could post it. Let me just say that they got into a fight. It exploded so much that Clint told Bill to fuck off and as he walked out said fuck this place. We never did get the whole story about what happed to make him say that to Bill but the bar didn't want him back. We figured we would talk to him at the show we were doing at Tree Top because he said he would do it with us.

Now Prime and his video were great. He found a song that fit his personality and during the first part of the song he did a very sexy dance. Then he took off his shirt and he was wearing tassel pasties and he made them spin to the song. It was perfect. It was a joke for Prime but that was his personality…so happy and full of laughter. He likes to make sure everyone is happy even at the expense of his own happiness. It was no surprise that he won the contest. We were so proud of him.

Prime's popularity now had him traveling a lot. He started doing club events for the company. The bar's loved him but the guys he traveled with not so much. They didn't want the other guys back to the clubs they only wanted Prime. Michael talked to him and told him what to watch out for. Remember Prime was fairly new to the whole gay club scene. He had done some shows with us and gogo'd a lot but now he was getting ready to enter into California Underwear Model gay world...where the sharks really bite.

Now you never get the respect you deserve in your own home town. Tree Top didn't start advertising until the week before. How do you expect to sell out a show without advertising? Well the attendance would be what you would expect. Most of the crowd just stumbled across the show because they happed to come in that night. There were some of our fans that traveled hours to see our show that night...actually there are several of our fans that travel wherever we go...it is nice. Now as far as the show it was great...with what we had to work with.

So the first problem was from Clint...the day before we talked but the day of...not a word. So with no surprise...he didn't show up. Drake told us a couple hours before the show he wasn't coming but that he was sending a replacement...which didn't show up either. So for the show all we had was Michael, Felipe, Hunter, Fernando and Sin...we put on a good show though even though it was shit from the start. On top of all the problems the bar also had a drag show going on...most people walking in came to see the drag show because they didn't know about our show. Sad...just sad... Michael needs people who will take it as serious as he does and that is hard to come by.

When people don't show up it looks bad on him...they take money away from my kids because people don't want us back and when they don't want us back we fall in the hole. There have been times when I asked Michael if enough was enough. We put our family in the hole for this group at times and it is hard when our daughter asks for things and I know I cannot give her what she needs. I was the only one working a job and it was hard. Things needed to change. Even with Michael... Sometimes I look at all the stuff Michael does to look young and all I can do is giggle. I make fun of him by saying it is sad my husband has more make-up than I do. I love the people in the group but it wasn't just about them. In business it is about making money. The money was good when we made it but with me the only one working it is hard. On a good note I was beginning to see the old Michael slowly coming back. Sadly it was because Felipe was not coming around so much. They really only saw each other when they danced. Felipe would drive down at night to talk to him sometimes but that couldn't happen a lot since Felipe had to get up early in the morning to go to work.

I saw the strain it had on Michael and Felipe but I had to focus on Michael and he was slowly coming back. It took a strain on us too because of Michael's frustrations. We had not been on a date in a long time and Michael told me he wanted to go out with Felipe for his birthday. That was ok but it was my birthday and our anniversary. I was not happy. Yes, Felipe needed time and he needed to be shown that he was cared about and to thank him for all that he has done for us but it was our anniversary and I told Michael that I had no problem with him doing that but we had to come first. That never happened…he went out with Felipe and we didn't have our anniversary for another two months. He told me he would just take the ass chewing he was going to get but after all Felipe had done he was going out with him I understood that he had done a lot for us but that was our time. We had been through a lot too and it seemed like that part of it was no big deal. Ok…there were a few steps back at times but when I started this I knew it was going to be a long road.

I should say that at this time Michael reached undetectable statues with his illness. What undetectable means is the illness is no longer in his blood stream. This also means it is less likely to pass it on to anyone. I am still illness free. Now this doesn't mean that he still doesn't carry the illness inside his body. The doctors say it usually hides in the lymph nodes. Like I said before there was an article done to where they followed a group of partners where one had the illness and the other didn't. In this test all the negative partners stayed negative even though they were not taking precautions to keep themselves negative. At the end of the study nobody came back positive except one and they had stepped out on their partner. Michael and I will always take precautions just because we have kids and can't afford $6000 a month for me to go on medication too.

How sad is that his meds cost $3000 a month? Can you say over kill? You cannot tell me the research lab has not already made their money back. They get grants and special interest funding and yet the pill, one pill, cost $100. Sadly they know we will pay it to stay alive but that is sad. I guess that is the American Dream…making money on the backs of others. Michael being undetectable is wonderful news though.

The guys were busy for the rest of the year between dancing at Chris's, Sidewinders and private parties. Halloween is always fun it is like gay Christmas because everyone goes all out for it. Michael, Drake and Hunter danced that year at Chris's. Hunter pulled together a very sexy nerd with fake glasses and all and a pumpkin outfit that showed off all of his assets. There was not much to it except a pumpkin mask covering his front that he had attached to a skimpy pair of underwear; he also wore green bands around his wrists with green socks. It looked really good.

Michael had made a Baron Sum De costume that year. He had taken an old leather jacket cut off the sleeves and turned it into a vest and sewed small bones in a crisscross design on it...well I sewed them on. He found a little skull that he put spikes from an old leather harness he had down the center of the skull and positioned it in the middle of a black hat and leather pants...now the pants come off to reveal his leather underwear.

Drake didn't really dress up when he gogo'ed. He just wore his regular stuff. This year he did pull together a cowboy type themed costume and a rocker type outfit. Chris's had put a big Frankenstein head decoration and the guys danced in front of the open mouth. A new bar contacted Michael around Halloween and wanted us out...yea a new bar!!

The next show was Ralph's first show with us. He looked nervous but it didn't take him long to find his footing. Michael also took Prime, Superman, Felipe and one of Felipe's friends. Now Felipe's friend was an odd one. When we picked him up he brought a girl with him...remember what happened with the last girl...but whatever. Now the car ride was odd because I sat up front with Felipe and normally Felipe didn't talk much to anyone in the car but this time he didn't stop talking. Everyone noticed... Felipe talked and laughed with his straight friend but didn't really talk to his group brothers...yea...we all thought that was odd. I knew Felipe was not comfortable with his bi side but I didn't really realize how much. He even told Michael that they were going to keep things on the quiet side about the two of them. Now...here is this guy who says he "loves" my husband but yet will not admit to people who he is...I am very proud to say Michael is my husband and if someone doesn't like his choices then I just tell them to fuck off. Michael actually brought this up to Felipe in the back of Chris's and told him everyone noticed Felipe's behavior and his response was that they were his friends...yea...that pissed off Michael and Prime...because the guys were the only ones who accepted Felipe…all of Felipe…for who he was. This was not the only issue that show had…with Felipe's friend. None of the people who came to the show liked him because he would walk over take their money and leave…without spending anytime with the people. I heard that more than one time and I heard it enough that I had to talk to Michael about it because he was making us look bad. Now the last thing was when I walked in the dressing room and I saw him walking away from Michael's bag…this really struck me as odd. Later I found out that Michael was missing money.

Now Superman brought a woman with him too but she was ok. She is older than he is and was getting a divorce. She started coming to all the shows Superman came to. She is a nice lady…a bit odd…but nice. She always got them a room but she came to the show and just hung out like someone is supposed to do. I have no problem there.

Now Ralph and Prime bonded at this show. Ralph remembers this show with pride. Prime taught Ralph that if you put your privates in there face they tip. Ralph loved Prime from that moment on. We all had a good time…especially the famous pie fight. It all started because Michael kept teasing Felipe about his sweet tooth. Felipe had bought pie at the restaurant we ate at to take with him. Michael kept talking about Felipe feeding his pie hole. When we got back to the hotel Michael said something like…look fatty is feeding his pie hole again…when Felipe stood up and shoved the pie in Michael's face. It was on from that second on. They chased each other all over the room smearing pie on each other. Pie was everywhere…except neither one of them got it on the white underwear they were wearing. Prime stepped out of the shower and just shook his head when he saw the two of them. Later we found out that poor Ralph had to listen to Felipe's friend and the girl go at it all night.

Back on the home front we were still booking private parties and doing gogo every weekend. I love going to Chris's and hanging out with my best friend Blake. A wonderful man named Paul would work at Blake's bar when he went to see his boyfriend. Paul is a tall and slender older man who for some odd reason keeps a rubber band around his wrist and pulls on it a lot letting it hit his wrist. I have never asked why he does that…maybe one day I will. I like him though he is easy to talk to and I find him very intelligent. I miss Blake when he leaves but I am glad that I have gotten to know Paul.

Every weekend we are in town you can find me at the end of the bar talking to Blake. He is doing very well in school. I know I could never take or do the classes he is doing. He has chosen the medical profession and he is very good at it. Also he and I have been talking about a new guy he has met. I think it is so cute because his face lights up when he talks about him. When I finally got to meet him...he is amazing. Just a good guy... not what I expected Blake to be with but they are so into each other and you can see the care for each other in their eyes. He came in and gave me a hug and just instantly stole my heart. I am so happy for Blake because he deserves happiness. Jimmy is the perfect match for Blake. His caring heart is only matched by his passion for Blake and life. I am glad the two met. Michael gets on to the two of us because he says we take to long at the end of the night because we are still talking. Blake was having issues with his family which really made him worry if they were going to be ok. Speaking about family...we got a text from one of Fernando's friends saying that he was deported.

Michael and I tried to get a hold of him to find out what was going on. After about a day we were able to find out that he had went to one of his appointments with our government and because he was late they deported him...this is what the friend told us. Now Fernando told us that was the case but he had talked to someone about rescheduling his appointment and they told him it was fine but that when he got there they put him in jail and deported him. For the next month the guys danced trying to raise money to help get him back to the states.

This put us down one dancer...not to mention we didn't know if we would be able to get him home because he had been living and working here...and he worked for me at the gas station for a bit too...for 10 years. Our government sucks...the red tape and stupid things it does to people who have been here for years being a vital part of the community. We knew that Fernando came from a small town and we worried about him because of all the violence we hear about how they treat gay people. We wanted him home where he belonged. I will say that the pictures he sent of where he comes from were some of the most beautiful pictures I have ever seen. Felipe went through some of this stuff a long time ago and he even tried talking to Fernando on Facebook. As we all know though the world doesn't stop...

so we were getting ready for a show coming up in March, two events, not to mention the private parties and dancing...so on with the world.

Felipe was wanted for a private gig. Michael told Felipe that he would take care of all the details because the guy had cancelled once already but Felipe said "I Got This"...which is one of Michael's irritation points because any time someone says that...they so don't...Got It. So Michael gets a text from Felipe the night of the gig asking Michael to call him and make up some excuse to get him out of the situation he had gotten himself in. Michael called and the excuse he came up with was that he needed to dance at Chris's. Felipe asked Michael if he could find someone else...which through Michael off because of the text. Michael was sitting on the couch with me and all I could see is Michael's face and he told Felipe that he didn't really have to dance but that was the excuse he was using to get him out of there. With an odd look on his face Michael said ok and hung up the phone. He told me that Felipe said he wanted to stay. Now we had just gotten the text and called him and now he wanted to stay...whatever. This confused us but we moved on. Now that weekend something happened between Michael and Felipe that really put things in perspective for Michael.

This guy had spent all this money and time on Felipe by getting him a massage, taking him out to eat and bought him all this underwear because he wanted to. Michael pointed out that Felipe must have liked it or he wouldn't have stayed. Now at this time Michael and Felipe were not spending that much time together because the old Michael was coming back and he was really busy with the group and the family...like he had been when they met. Now my take on what happened was a way for Felipe to let Michael know that he needed to spend more time with him and show him that he cared... and attempt to I guess maybe make him jealous but not jealous...of course I never said anything to Michael because the old Michael is a straight forward person and if you need or want something you just tell him. Michael did care about Felipe and tried to show him but our family didn't have money to just throw around. When Michael pointed out the fact that Felipe must have liked all the attention from this guy it pissed Felipe off. Michael told Felipe that he was going to have a cig and then they could leave because he wasn't getting anything out of Felipe.

When Michael came back in Felipe was gone. Michael gathered up his stuff and walked out of the bar only to see Felipe driving away. Felipe got stopped at the red light and Michael walked over and still on the sidewalk through up his hands as if to say…WTF…and walked back to the front door of the bar. Felipe just went on. Felipe was Michael's ride and he just left him there with no ride home. Michael was sitting on the ½ wall at the end of the building for 10 minutes pissed trying to figure out how to get home when Felipe pulled back in the parking lot. Michael stood up and got in the car. Michael told him that he would have never done that to Felipe. He explained it that when you "love" someone you don't leave them. He said that no matter how mad he would have been at me or me at him neither one of us would have left the other. He compared the situation to a cartoon of this old man who looks mad as hell holding an umbrella over his wife while he sits in the rain. That was Michael's turning point and he was back to what he knew all along to what was most important…his family. He understood that his family needed him to be back to where he was. Sadly he also knew that this was his and Felipe's turning point and things would never be the same.

When he got home and told me what had happened I was mad. I knew you didn't do that to someone you love but I didn't really have to say anything because Michael was saying it all for me. I could see it on his face and in his eyes that he was in the doorway. I was so happy to see the fire back in his eyes…there is my Zeus.

New Year's Eve was the next event for the group. Michael took Felipe and Prime to a little bar that after talking to me didn't want to book but Michael talked to them…because he was a man…they booked the guys to come down. You know that really bothered me…I talk the guys up…tell everyone they are all gay or bi…I tell them to look at the website and our Facebook page but I get nothing…total Bullshit. Anyway…Michael talked to him and booked the guy for their New Year's Eve event. I didn't go because I wanted to stay home with our youngest. I told Michael to have fun and stick to our agreement. We had agreed that I was the only one that he would wake up next to…which meant he was not to sleep with Felipe. Now I don't know if they did or didn't all I know is that Michael say they didn't.

Prime cleaned up that night making $500-$600 that night and Felipe and Michael did well also. Hey everyone that is what the guys should be making. They work hard…but I have already ranted about that…so the guys had fun that night and Michael came home with an interesting story about one of the guys that came to see them. We will just refer to him as the biter. Yes…I said biter. This time he got Prime which sent Prime to the moon. He shows up and tries to bite all of them.

The beginning of the year started out on the run. First Prime was spending a lot of time on the road between California, New York and Florida. The contest he won put him on the fast track between photo shoots…video's…and bar gigs he was flying. We were so proud of him when Chris's played a video that had Prime in it. Little did we know at the time what a hard time Prime was really having. Remember when I said he took a lot of things to heart…well…he was swimming with sharks now that didn't care about him. He always put on his game face but underneath he would be in turmoil. When we would see him he always told us things were great but I noticed there was something about him that was off but when he wasn't opening up there was nothing any of us could do. We loved him and I was worried.

Mandy contacted Michael again about another fashion show. I went to one of the fittings she was having. Lisa, Michael's sister, went with us because she was going to try her hand at modeling. Standing 5'5" runway was a bit of a stretch for her but she was beautiful and her face belonged on a runway. We also took our two daughters and grandbaby. Our oldest thought she might want to start modeling too. Our youngest chanced the baby around but all the baby wanted was me or Papaw. She was so damn cute. Our youngest loved the wings Mandy was doing and wished she was old enough to model. John, Lisa's boyfriend…that we liked…also came. He is a lot of fun to be around. His look is a lot like Mr. Glass which is funny….I love Mr. Glass so it would only seem right to love his younger clone. No John is a supper nice guy who treats Lisa like gold and we are lucky to have him in the family.

So Ralph, Felipe, Drake, and Stone were all supposed to meet us there. Stone never showed up for the fitting. I will take a minute out of this story to tell you about Stone. Michael met him at Chris's one night. Stone is of Italian decent so he has dark hair and eyes and his body was tight. He was around our age but kept up on his body not like most guys our age. Very nice guy and good personality…he did have a fatal flaw…he was a bit of a flake. What I mean by that is he is not dependable…he says he wants to do stuff but there is no follow through. So like I said he told us he would be there and never showed up. So I watched Drake try to get an outfit to fit over his thighs…it was a no go. Drake's thighs were massive so Mandy had a hard time with him. Felipe didn't really like the clothing choice Mandy had for him but like a trooper he put it all on. Michael and Ralph did not care what they had to wear. I heard Mandy talk about how she needed help and I volunteered.

The night of the show I realized that Mandy was a bit disorganized. She didn't have her runway music which she asked me to figure out. I said ok but needed to know the theme of her show and she said she didn't know so I looked at all the outfits and picked the music. Ralph and I stood around outside laughing together about the people we were seeing looking for music. I love hanging out with him he is so personable. So the show itself went well…there were a lot of adjusting, fixing, and changing something at the last second. Mandy was still making some of the outfits while we were waiting to go on. All in all it was a good show. I get so proud of my husband and my guys when I get to watch the things they do.

The next event was a video premier by a local artist who has gone global in the club circuit. Michael has known him for about 5 years. So when Michael got a message from him that he wanted to do the premier of his new video at Chris's Michael was all for it. Ryan W. had been performing in Europe and came home to make his video to his song, "Hardcore". Michael asked Prime, Felipe and Drake to help. Ryan W. had them come up to Chris's for a run through of what was going to happen the night of the premier. Now the things I heard from the general populous stood true to form that you are never as popular in your hometown as you are everywhere else. I find it funny though everyone who talked bad were front row center… so they showed up just to say something bad…if I don't like something I avoid it. Anyway Ryan W. bought the guys outfits to wear that night and gold hair spray to fit with what he was doing. The guys were to carry him from the back to where he would "sing" raised above their heads. When they lowered him down he was standing in front of a large cross. After the video was over the Boyz gogo'ed and I got some amazing pictures of Prime and Michael together. It was a fun night.

Oh…I should add something here because we found out what happened to the Canadian. Michael saw that his Facebook had changed so he sent him a message. The reply he got back was something else. Now before I go on let me tell you if it had been anyone else I would not have believed it but because it was him I believed it all. Also I should say now it is when we found out… yes it has been this long. So on with his story. Ok so first he told Michael that when he left us he ran into a girl who invited him to a frat party…free alcohol…oh yea he agreed to go. Well something happened while he was there because he said he got into a fight with the fraternity…yes I said the whole fraternity. One guy picked him up and threw him through a table. I guess it was a good thing because he was able to use one of the legs to defend himself. He said after that he wondered around and found himself on the roof of a building. He said he slept up there and when he woke up he said he fell through the roof. After a wild night and a shitty morning he said he just called a cab and went home. Wow…but we were glad to finally hear from him and it was nice to know he was still alive.

Michael was also at this time working with Sin on her burlesque show that she does every year. This year she wanted to incorporate the Boyz. No other burlesque group had masculine well-built men performing with them. Michael was all for it. Felipe was in too because he loved the theater. Actually Felipe was more comfortable doing that type of performing. We will get into everything that happened later because I need to talk about our next show.

Michael and Felipe talked about an opening number for the group and Michael asked Felipe to come up with a number routine. So that weekend when Michael asked Felipe if the number was done he told Michael that he had it and was working on it. Michael told me that he was nervous because of what Felipe had said. That weekend was filled with surprises. 1st wonderful surprise was Roco. I walked past this amazing looking man with a smile to die for…he stopped me in my tracks. I talked to him about dancing. He told me he was nervous to dance but I could see it in his eyes that he would love it. After a few weekends I finally talked him into it and once he was on the box he loved it. Roco stands about 6'2" with dark chocolate smooth skin and built like nobody's business. One thing I always hear about him besides his amazing smile, rippling muscles is his ass…you could bounce a quarter off of it. He has this way of making you think he is so sweet and innocent with his smooth way of talking but the minute he starts biting his lip and gives someone that look his true identity comes out…but that is for another time. The 2nd thing was that Fernando's ex-boyfriend wanted to dance with the group. Rei was short thinner built but built for his size. He has an odd speech pattern but he puts everything he has into what he does... so Michael gave him a shot even though he knew the problems Rei just came from. Michael asked Rei to come to the next show we were about to do.

The first practice to get ready for the show Felipe had not come up with anything which pissed Michael off. Felipe did not understand why Michael was so mad and I explained it to him. Michael was walking through the door of being the old Michael and that was something everyone was going to have to get used to. I know he has a large personality which is something Felipe was not used to the new attitude. Michael went out to smoke to cool off. Michael came back and between the two they came up with really nothing so Michael just decided to do a number he had done before.

This show was special because our oldest went with us. This was going to be the first time she would ever see her dad perform. Michael had brought Rei, Felipe, Ralph, Prime and Stone. We had planned the show as if Stone was not going to show up but it was a relief when he did. Stone road with us to the show. Now once we got there it was odd because I asked Felipe where he wanted to sleep figuring that we would figure out something because our daughter had come but he just walked by me and put his stuff down on the bed Stone had put his stuff on. I just shook my head and walked back to our room and told our daughter that the bed was all hers because Felipe was staying in the other room. So Samantha invited us over to their room to partake in some natural cigs before the show. Rei and Ralph went over to "relax" before the show although from what we heard there was not a lot of relaxing. Let us just say that the relaxing and smile was not from the cig they had put in their mouth it was the body parts.

So with the show getting ready to start I took our daughter and asked her to video the first number because I needed to let the guys know when they needed to go out. She was cool with that. So I walked back made sure they all looked good and we started the show. When the opening number was over which is just a tease for the audience to get a little peek at the men headed their way. I made my way back out to my daughter. When I got there I noticed she had tears in her eyes. As a mom I got very concerned because my daughter was crying. I was worried someone did or said something to her but that was not the case. She looked at me after I asked if she was ok and with the biggest smile she said, "That's my dad". I could see from her expression she was so proud of her dad. Now I know that he is a stripper so most just rolled your eyes but he does put on one hell of a show. Her smile and glow made me tear up...which it is hard to take pictures with tears in your eyes but anyway.

Now my daughter had her eye on Ralph. She was so taken by him it was cute. As the show was winding down she came and sat down beside me and told me that she could deal with someone being bi. I just looked at her and said it is not as easy as we make it look and that I knew Ralph was a wonderful man who has become part of our family but that she needed to be sure. Also, Felipe was very quiet and stuck right by Stone's side. I found that odd.

The only issue we had that weekend was with the drag queens coming back to where the guys were dressing. Our daughter said she saw one of them looking in someone's bag. There is one thing I cannot stand is a thief. I am sorry that you didn't make any tips maybe you should look at yourself and what you can do to make more money. The rest of the night I or my daughter stayed in the back with all the stuff.

Now it was time to leave. Stone decided to ride with Felipe and Ralph rode with us...which was fine by us because we love Ralph. We had a blast on the way home. Our daughter flirted almost all the way home...sadly he played for the other team and that is where he was going to stay. It was cute to watch though. Now when we got home things turned weird.

Michael and Felipe didn't really talk for two days. Sure there was...good mornings...or the very occasional...hey...through-out the day but neither of them really talked to each other. After 2 weeks had gone by Felipe called Michael and asked if he could come down because he needed to talk to him. When he showed up Michael went out to his car to talk to him and I went to bed. I had not fallen asleep yet when I heard him come back in so I got up to see what was going on. When I asked him what was going on he told me that Felipe told him that he had fallen out of love with him because they didn't spend time together as much as they did and that all they do is fight and argue anymore. Michael said he asked him why they argued and let him know it was because he didn't share things with him...things would happen and he wouldn't let Michael know for 2 or 3 days...Michael would say hey let's go do "whatever" and then he would find out that Felipe would have made plans with his family 2 weeks ago...this is why they argued. Felipe also told Michael that he and Stone had a lot in common and it was easy to talk to him about things. Michael told him that there was only one thing they had in common because Stone was out and didn't have to hide anything but Felipe was not. He also pointed out that they had only met during the show...now they stayed in the room and didn't eat or hang with the rest of us but how well can you get to know someone with others around. Felipe said he was attracted to him. After Michael told me all this I could see the hurt in his eyes so I told him that how can someone just fall out of love with someone over those reasons...also that Felipe had never met Stone but he picked to stay in the other room without finding out if he could have even stayed in our room.

See I knew Michael was not distant because he was busy with the group and that was the old Michael. Neither I or Michael maintenance friends very well...sometimes one has to tell the other they want attention and we are married living in the same house...sleeping in the same bed. This was Michael again...this was normal behavior for Michael.

After sometime Michael told Felipe that he was coming up to see him because they had not been talking and things about the conversation bothered Michael. He knew Felipe was not telling the truth and Michael wanted to get to the bottom of it. Michael had thought before that if I had died or left Felipe was the only one that he ever thought he might be able to have a relationship with...or if things got really bad between Michael and I and more open between the two of them that he would try a relationship between the two of them. Michael knows that when you love someone you work at things to make things work because you love the other person so he couldn't wrap his head around what Felipe was saying.

Michael went to the gym Felipe worked at to talk to him...they had talked a bit on the phone but Michael felt that in person would be better. When they began talking Michael brought up some of the things Felipe had talked about and told him that Stone was out what was going to happen when Stone outed him...because Felipe was not out at all. Stone was out and wouldn't deal with the behaviors Felipe had by not being out. Michael pointed out that the grass is not always greener on the other side because Michael wouldn't out him because Michael wasn't out except to the group and the clubs. Michael also pointed out that the one thing they had in common Michael had always been supportive about and that just because he had not been through it to the degree Felipe had he still understood and was trying to help him through it. He also told him that they had more in common so that wasn't the reason this was going on. Michael wanted Felipe to be honest with him and not just make excuses. Michael also explained that things were calming down and time was going to be opening up for them. Michael had always told Felipe that if he met someone…figuring it would be a woman…he would understand and would be supportive. Michael saw the look on Felipe's face and he knew that he was upset because he was angry and hurt and a bit of self-loathing but Michael needed the truth. Felipe finally admitted that he still loved Michael but that he was tired of being alone. He said that he wanted Michael to stay over sometimes or maybe take a trip with him but understood that would never happen. Michael explained that those things might happen down the road but no not right at this moment.

When Michael got home he told me that he didn't like what was going on but it was nice that he finally was honest with him. I felt bad that things ended and I took some blame for that because of what I was doing trying to help Michael get back to his old self. I felt bad that I couldn't tell them what was going on because I knew at this moment Michael would have been mad at me but I knew later when I told him he would understand and agree with what I did. My heart was breaking for both of them. I wish Felipe could have just hung out a bit longer because Michael was almost back to being him.

I think I will stop the story here…yes there is more…a lot more…but that is for next time. I wrote this book because I have enjoyed my life even with all the issues. I also want the world to know that it takes all kinds of people to make this world go around. Gay people are just like everyone else. My friends have given me so much joy and excitement. Who cares who they take home or fall in love with let them be!! People look at Michael and me and say we are odd and that we don't fit together but I would put our relationship up against anyone's. We have more love for each other than most people.

For all those women who will find out that their husbands are stepping out a few words of wisdom. Think about things before you react. Not all men are dogs and some of them actually have a glitch. A glitch is something that can be worked through. All it takes is commitment from both and a lot of love and patients. They lie because in their head they feel they are saving your feelings and what they do doesn't change the way they feel about you. They love you to the ends of the earth. They lie because they are scared to lose what they have. They feel that if you don't know you are better off. There are others that need to be kicked to the curb but the good ones lose everything and so do you. Think is it worth throwing everything away for one or two days a year, I don't hence why we are still together going strong.

I would never want to lose my best friend, lover, father to my kids, and my hero because of one or two days a year. Some of you may say that I am crazy but I am here to tell you I am not. Well I am crazy for him. Without him I wouldn't have met all my brothers who dance with Michael. I wouldn't have made the wonderful friends I now have in my life. All of them have brought great joy to my life. This is only the beginning of my story trust me there is more but I think that is enough drinks for now.

I hope that everyone reading this takes away a few things. Life is how you want to see it. For those of you who are closed minded and see sin everywhere and in everything maybe you will become more tolerant because you know you should not worry about the splinter in my eye but the timber in your own.

For the women who find out that your husband is stepping out how does that really change your life? You knowing is the only change. He has been doing this for some time and you never knew so what does it really change. You need to ask yourself some questions. Does it really change how he feels about you? Is losing everything you have built together worth throwing away for one or two days a year? Is there anyway the two of you can work things out without losing everything? How much do you really love him because loving all of him was what you signed on for?

Those of you who thought dancers or strippers are dirty social degenerates now you understand it is just a job. Dancers/Strippers live their lives out in the open so who is more dirty the one who has 12 kids by 12 different dads or the man who doesn't know how many kids he has because he doesn't support any of them or the entertainers who leave it all at the box and go home and get a good night's sleep alone.

Those of you who read this because you wanted the dirt I hope you understand that drama only causes problems. Those who spread drama are just trouble makers. If I listened to all the drama makers Michael and I would have never even gotten together. How about before you try and ruin other people's lives you try and fix your own life.

If you look at our history there is always someone or some group being persecuted. Why is that? Why can't we all just grow as a group of people understanding that we are all people? Why do we have to have someone to fight especially when the group that is being persecuted just wants what everyone else already has? As humans we all believe that what we want and what we believe is the best but that doesn't mean we need to cram it down the throats of those who don't feel the same way. Imagine what we could do as a nation if we all put aside our differences and really went after problems that affect us all…poverty, violence, child abuse, the homeless population, healthcare, the elderly…there are far better battles to be fought than each other. Why do we all have to fight over things that don't really matter?

Till Next Time…. Enjoy what you have. Love the one you're with. Make the best of every day. Live your life to the fullest. Talk to you soon and maybe we will have another drink and I will tell you more.

Printed in the United States
By Bookmasters